Contents

Editorial

'Perhaps for the first time since the 1930s, the phenomena of unemployment and poverty have become common to both the developed and developing countries'
(Bhalla and Lapeyre 1997, 421).

While rapid change to the pattern of trade and industrial production is transforming the global economy and challenging North–South differences in the way women and men experience employment (Hale 1996), Northern governments and non-governmental organisations (NGOs) are debating the role of the state in continuing to provide a welfare safety net[1] for all its citizens, and discussing alternative means of working to eradicate poverty and meet basic needs.

Increasingly, international development policy-makers and practitioners are becoming involved in debates with governments and NGOs in the North, about appropriate methods of understanding and tackling Northern poverty. Until recently, mainstream social policy and practice to address poverty in the industrialised countries (often referred to as 'Northern'), and 'development' work which takes place in 'Southern' countries, have tended to remain conceptually distinct from each other, and little cross-fertilisation has taken place between the two disciplines and policy arenas.

In line with this new focus on finding solutions for Northern poverty in the experience of the South, for the first time, *Gender and Development* is devoting an issue to the topic of poverty and gender relations in various Northern contexts. The authors of the articles in this collection were asked to consider the differences and similarities between experiences of poverty as it relates to gender identity, in different 'Northern' and 'Southern' contexts, and to consider how sharing perspectives on approaches to poverty reduction in these different contexts might be mutually enriching.

The 'South in the North'

As Peggy Antrobus of DAWN (Development Alternatives with Women for a New Era) has observed: 'the terms North and South ... need to be examined ... there is a "South" in the North ... and there is a "North" in the South ... many of us [working in gender and development] are in fact members of that class' (Antrobus 1993, 10). There is a danger that labels such as 'South' and 'North' can, by grouping together diverse countries and regions, obscure the very real differences between them.

If industrialised countries do not form a monolithic 'North', neither can women living in poverty be seen as a homogenous group. In particular, discrimination on grounds of race and ethnicity interlocks with that based on gender, to disadvantage women from racial minorities.

While Peggy Antrobus used the phrase 'South in the North' to describe all communities living in poverty, the phrase is also often used to describe those people, living temporarily or permanently in Northern contexts, whose ethnic roots, or nationality, are Southern. Many women from Southern contexts work as migrant workers in the North (WIDE 1995); they may experience a sense of isolation, exploitation and marginalisation from the host society. The experiences of women migrant workders will be included in articles in the next issue of Gender and Development, in March 1998, which focuses on migration.

Gender, women's poverty, and social exclusion

The concept of 'social exclusion' is becoming well-known in debates in the NGO sector in industrialised countries (Bhalla and Lapeyre 1997). This form of exclusion can be defined as the inability to attain a basic standard of living and participate in the 'major social and occupational institutions of the society — [including] employment, housing, health care, [and] education' (UN 1995, 15). The idea of 'social exclusion' is reminiscent of the concept of women's poverty in gender and development theory and practice, which emphasises that poverty does not only have an economic dimension, but is also concerned with people's exclusion from social and political participation and decision-making in institutions including the family, the market, and the state (Kabeer 1995).

Countering stereotypes of poverty in the North

Many people in industrialised and industrialising countries alike share a perception of the North as, quite simply, affluent; yet this stereotype is as over-simplistic as images of Africans as constantly hungry. A second misconception is that in Northern countries, the existence of state support means universal provision of basic necessities; thus, 'true' poverty does not exist in the North (for a discussion of this and other myths, see National Food Alliance 1997). In fact, as Sara Chamberlain's article discusses in the US context, state welfare payments are far from adequate to meetg the needs of women, men and children living in poverty, and the value of such benefits is rapidly eroding.

In addition, as Sara Chamberlain explores in her article on North American poverty, living in a state where many people are affluent places extreme pressure on poor people who are stigmatised as being inadequate and unsuccessful, and whose lack of spending power leads to social as well as economic exclusion. While poverty may not be life-threatening in most cases in the North, gross income inequalities within a society may pressurise poor people into making choices between meeting basic needs, and living as a socially-accepted member of that society. 'In a modern social democracy, with conspicuously wealthy sections of the population, people may be unwilling to accept ... severely limited diets ... it's not easy eating very low-cost diets when you live in a take-away, convenience culture, with intensive TV advertising... cheap, dull food is socially excluding' (National Food Alliance 1997, 11).

In an environment where many believe poverty is due to laziness or inadequacy on the part of the poor themselves, countering such negative imagery is a critical aspect of anti-poverty work. In her article, Tessa Swithinbank discusses street newspapers as a strategy for addressing the problems faced by men and women living on the streets in the UK, Eastern Europe, and South Africa: vendors can earn a living and establish a link with wider society, while selling a product which educates readers on the causes of homelessness and shows that poverty is not caused by personal moral failing but by political, economic and social structures.

Changing employment patterns for women and men

Over the past 25 years, discussions about equality for women have hinged on access to the links between income-earning and power relations between women and men, and the division of labour between the sexes within the home (Folbre 1994). Women's ability to participate in paid employment or income generation outside the home is affected by their responsibilities to children and other dependents. Thus, as in the South, globalisation and liberalisation have a different impact on Northern women and on Northern men, according to their roles and social context. For example, while in some situations women are finding they are required to participate more in the workforce, in low-paid precarious jobs, in other situations, for example in Spain (which has the lowest level of women's economic activity in Western Europe), women are the first to lose their employment as public-spending cuts are imposed (WIDE 1995).

Self-employment and micro-finance

Self-employment through the provision of microfinance has been seen in Southern, and increasingly in Northern, contexts as a potential solution to women's under-employment, low pay, and job insecurity. The current huge international interest in microfinance as a 'magic bullet' to end poverty reflects awareness of the success of large-scale initiatives in the South including that of the Grameen Bank in Bangladesh.

As Ruth Pearson and Erika Watson highlight in their article on the Full Circle project, a micro-finance project for women in the east of England, there is a perceived link in the popular imagination between poverty, lack of education, and poor employment prospects. However, in reality it is the inability of mothers living in poverty (with or without partners) to escape the poverty trap of low wages and high child-care costs which typically militates against their coming off benefits and gaining employment. The Full Circle Project has been designed after research in the United States and with knowledge of credit interventions in Southern countries. Knowledge from these sources indicates the importance of understanding women's activities in entrepreneurship and at home as interlinked. In Northern countries, women need to be able to embark on a business venture without losing their right to state welfare support for their families. The Full Circle Project experience indicates that the welfare system needs to be adapted to accommodate, not hinder, women from taking calculated risks in the first stages of entrepreneurship.

The role that income generation has in increasing women's self-confidence and sense of power is highlighted in Annette Rimmer's article focusing on the links between provision of credit through Community Credit Unions, and women's empowerment in many aspects of their lives: their relationships with their marital partners, within the community, and with external institutions including banks and potential employers.

Women, caring, rights, and obligations

Cross-cultural discussions about family life often depict stereotypes of industrialised Northern countries as regions where close family ties have broken down, and there is a culture which stresses the virtues of individualism. It is true that discussions about family obligations versus valuing the rights of the individual are familiar terrain for feminists in the North; yet, for most women in the North, just as for women in the South, the question is how to balance the emotional and practical demands of family members with their own needs and priorities (Elliot 1996). Feminist economists have argued that in order to change the value society places on reproductive work, and to release women from the trap of poverty or dependency on a male breadwinner, their work should be valued in national accounts; and some have argued that women should receive 'wages for housework' (Lewenhak 1992).

Racist and sexist stereotypes are commonly invoked to explain the different attitudes of various communities, families and individual people to 'family values' and the rights of individuals. In some cases in Northern contexts, these stereotypes have been used by social policy-makers to justify lack of statutory provision of care for elderly and disabled people. Such truisms as 'Asian families look after their own' are used as 'an excuse for institutions to provide the black and migrant community with less support than perceived "indigenous" women' (European Parliament, 1995, 94).

'Lone motherhood': separating fact from fiction

It is certainly true that household structures are changing; in Austria and Germany, at least one in every three households is single-person. The Northern stereotype of the nuclear family, with married parents and loving grandparents who live close by, belies the current proliferation of alternative family forms (Elliot 1996).

The UN 1995 publication *The World's Women* expresses the increased likelihood that children in Northern countries will spend at least part of their childhood in a lone-parent family as follows: '[in developed regions] people are marrying later or not at all, and marriages are less stable. Remarriage rates have dropped — especially for women — and lone-parent families now make up 10–25 per cent of all families' (UN, 1995, xix).

However, statistics like this need to be used with care; first, they mask a complex reality which varies from context to context: in southern parts of Europe where traditional family ties appear to have remained stronger, for example, Spain and Portugal, the figure is one in seven (UN 1995, 12). Second, such statistics are often cited in explanations of the causes of poverty which

focus on perceived family breakdown, demonising 'single mothers' and emphasising cultural, rather than political or economic, factors. Focusing on a cultural explanation for the problems faced by women living in poverty, and delinking these from the economic and political context, allows policy-makers to deny that they should play a role in seeking solutions.

In fact, the phrase 'lone motherhood' can cloak very different economic and social circumstances. For example, in the UK context, while almost one in every three births occurs outside marriage, half of these are within the context of co-habitation (Elliot 1996, 22). However, it is undeniable that social pressures on women to remain in marriages in which they are not happy have weakened in the past 30 years in the North. Divorce rates are highest in the US and Scandinavia, where one in every two marriages ends in divorce (UN, 1995, 11). Female-headed households present problems for the state welfare system since they oblige it to subsidise — and in so doing to recognise — the social and economic costs of bringing up children (Folbre 1994).

Addressing 'male exclusion'

'Solo parenthood, together with the contraction and casualisation of male labour markets, is evoking fears of men's redundancy and a growing sense that masculinity is in crisis' (Elliot 1996, 220). Changes in employment and patterns of family life are currently obliging social policy-makers in the North to address the issues of 'male exclusion' and how the loss of the role of breadwinner affects men's behaviour in their families and within wider society. An example of social policy work to address problems faced by young men is given in the interview in this issue, with Helen Carmichael of LEAP, an organisation working on conflict resolution and issues of crime among young offenders — predominantly male — in the UK context.

In this area of work, international development agencies have an opportunity to learn in their turn from Northern work and research, to identify how best to integrate masculinity and male exclusion into the GAD approach to development, which has tended to avoid problematising men and masculinity, preferring to focus on women as agents of social change and development (*Gender and Development* 5:2, 1997).

Changing demographics: old age as a gender issue

A major difference between the Northern and Southern contexts is that most countries in the South have a predominantly youthful population, whereas Northern societies are getting older: in 1990–95, 15 countries had a life expectancy of 80 years or more for women and 19 countries are expected to reach that level in 2000–05 (UN 1995, 66). Poverty is particularly likely for older women in countries with welfare systems based on contributions made while in employment, since many women have opted out of making regular contributions due to caring responsibilities (Elliot 1996).

Culturally, old age interacts with gender considerations to create particular difficulties for older women in societies which are male-dominated and celebrate youth. Post-menopausal women do not tend to be celebrated for their wisdom as may happen in non-industrial societies (Sen 1995); post-industrial societies value notions of 'progress', and constantly-evolving technologies and changes in the workplace mean that to keep 'up-to-date' is seen as more important than possessing knowledge based on years of experience. Attitudes to ageing are a dilemma for feminism, since stressing the onerous role of caring for old people, which typically falls to women, leads to negative stereotyping of older women as passive and socially and economically redundant (Sen 1995, Elliot 1996).

Learning lessons from women's international work against poverty

It has been strongly argued by many Southern gender and development practitioners and activists in the women's movement — including Fatma Alloo in her article with Wendy Harcourt in this issue — that only when their Northern counterparts gain experience through working on poverty in their own context can they understand the commonalities which exist between experiences of poverty in North and South. This first-hand experience cuts through racist and other stereotypes concerning the causes of poverty and will lead to a more mature understanding of the work to be done, and who is most equipped to perform it.

An important issue for women's movements in countries including Britain has been 'identity politics' in multi-racial societies. 'What keeps white women, who have done so much work on sexist power structures and regimes, their mechanisms and women's position within them, from an equally energetic and self-critical dialogue on racism?...we cannot fight for joint goals if we are not aware of our internalised oppression and dominance tendencies and the guilt they inspire' (WIDE 1995, 50). Alliances between women from South and North to fight common causes and symptoms of poverty need to be built on an acknowledgement of the ways in which white Northern women have greater power and privilege than women from ethnic minorities (WIDE 1995).

Bringing participatory methods from the South

Northern social policy work is currently learning from international development experience in the field of participatory research methods. These enable communities themselves to facilitate processes of research and identification of concerns in their own areas. 'People's participation is both a methodology and a strategic goal of development ... it is an alternative model which proposes both to improve people's standards of living and to give them a measure of control over the standards themselves' (Connell 1997, 251). Several articles in this issue discuss participatory methods of action research, used to identify issues and stimulate community groups into designing and enacting solutions. One in particular recounts in detail the process of a participatory Community Assessment in the UK. Ros David and Yvonne Craig, who facilitated the process, observe that 'in many contexts in the South, poor people themselves are progressively more involved in analysing their own situation and seeking ways to address their concerns. The process of supporting people as they address issues of social exclusion, low self-esteem, and voicelessness, has become central to NGO work.'

Identifying appropriate roles for different actors

Debates on learning about Southern experiences of poverty reduction are taking place against a backdrop of recognition in many Northern contexts that the state must link with other institutions to provide a holistic strategy to combat poverty. As in international development, debates in Northern social policy circles have highlighted the role of civil society, the private sector, and, critically, the NGO ('voluntary') sector. It is particularly important for the state to promote a climate which is friendly to institutional growth and change: 'voluntary organisations, it seems, are generally robust and adaptable plants but they do require supportive and hospitable environments if they are to thrive' (Harris 1997, 2).

A key issue for future work is to share learning between those involved in Northern development work: local authorities, regional government, and voluntary agencies (May 1997). Project design, fundraising, and implementation are complex processes

which often involve many different groups of people. This complexity has implications for South:North learning and cross-fertilisation on ostensibly similar issues, as the structures through which projects happen differ so radically (Patel 1996). Networks of organisations and individuals working around specific issues are proliferating; Tilly Sellers discusses the Hull and East Yorkshire PRA Network from the UK in her article in the Resources section. The implications of such structures are explored by many researchers into Northern initiatives. For example, in the UK context, the new Single Regeneration Budget run by government requires project proposals which cut across traditional sectoral divides, and 'may result in a more holistic improvement for the urban communities concerned' (Peace 1997, 252).

Southern and Northern women's organisations have been involved in lengthy campaigning, advocacy and joint research. These activities are based on the understanding that globalisation demands analyses and strategies which understand the similar causes of poverty worldwide; yet they also, crucially, recognise the different ways in which global trends interlock with regional conditions, to create specific effects.

References

Antrobus P (1993), Introduction to Young G, Samarasinghe V and Kusterer K *Women at the Center: Development Issues and Practices for the 1990s*, Kumarian Press.

Beall J (1997), 'Valuing difference and working with diversity' in Beall J (ed), *A City for All: Valuing Difference and Working with Diversity*, Zed Books:London

Bhalla A and Lapeyre F (1997), 'Social exclusion: towards an analytical and operational framework', *Development and Change* 28, Blackwell.

Connell D (1997), 'Participatory development: an approach sensitive to class and gender', *Development in Practice* 7:3, Oxfam.

Elliot F N (1996), *Gender, Family and Society*, Macmillan.

European Parliament (1995) *Confronting the Fortress: Black and Migrant Women in the European Union* ed. Subhan A, European Parliament Working Papers

Folbre N (1994), *Who pays for the kids? Gender and structures of constraint*, Routledge.

Hale A (1996), 'The deregulated global economy: women workers and strategies of resistance', *Gender and Development* 4:3, Oxfam.

Harris M (1997) *The Jewish Voluntary Sector in the United Kingdom: Its Role and its Future*, Institute for Jewish Policy Research:London.

Kabeer, N (1995), *Reversed Realities*, Verso.

Lewenhak S *The Re-valuation of Women's work*, Earthscan:London 1992

May N (1997) *Challenging Assumptions: Genmder Considerations in Urban Regeneration in the United Kingdom*, Joseph Rowntree Foundation.

National Food Alliance (1997), *Myths About Food and Low Income*, National Food Alliance.

Patel S (1997), 'People and Poverty: a look into community involvement in the process of community regeneration in the UK, sharing ideas and practice from working with slum communities in India', unpublished, Centre for Innovation in Voluntary Action/Oxfam UK/I.

Peace S (1997), 'The Single Regeneration Budget and Urban Planning in Oxford' in Beall J (ed), op cit.

Sen K (1995), 'Gender, culture, and later life: a dilemma for contemporary feminism', *Gender and Development* 3:3, Oxfam.

WIDE 1995 *Living and Working: An Illustration of the Feminisation of Poverty in Europe*, ed. Macdonald M, WIDE:Brussels

United Nations, *The World's Women 1995: Trends and Statistics*, UN 1995.

Note

1 The 'welfare state' has, in many countries of the North, provided a 'safety net' for all citizens, meeting a list of basic needs (including food, shelter, health and education).

From the South to the North:

evolving perspectives on gender and poverty

Fatma Alloo and Wendy Harcourt

How do women from the North and women from the South view gender and poverty? What are the differences and the similarities? In this article, we give our opinions as two women who have often shared platforms, representing those two identities of 'Southern' and 'Northern'; however, as we explain, we now question such categorisation.

The terms 'Northern' and 'Southern' are used in many ways. Perhaps the most obvious is Northern to refer to the industrial economies and Southern to the agricultural-based economies. Implicit in this definition is Northern countries as culturally and economically dominating, and Southern as economically and culturally colonised. Northerners are seen as the rich consumers, or the 'military mighty', and Southerners as the 'poor exploited': as the puppets caught up in the game.

Even if there is some truth in these characterisations, such categorisation can lead to a gross over-simplification of a very complex set of dynamics. Within such a polarisation, whole groups of people are forgotten or their identities blurred. Where, for example do the people of the CEEC (Central and East European Countries) belong? And what about indigenous peoples?

In the same way that feminists question the dualism of men versus women (Harcourt, 1994), we also have to break the dualism of North versus South and try to see the similarities among peoples, which cross geographic and cultural boundaries; especially in the context of globalisation, and debates on the demise of nation states. The growing poverty of many people, including women, is not geographically fixed, nor are the reasons for poverty. It is this shift in understanding, and the dynamics which produced such a shift, which we wish to explore.

For the purpose of this article we have tentatively kept to the definitions of North and South in their most obvious sense of geographical location, and the consequent political and economic situation women find themselves facing 'at home'. We should stress that we do not wish to suggest a commonality of voices among all women in the North or in the South! The interest in poverty and gender, among the women's groups we mention here, grew from different experiences and ideological positions: a liberal rights perspective, socialist feminist interests, eco-feminism, and cultural feminism; all of which have adherents in North and South.

What we have tried to share is our own experiences as women working with two different networks which situated themselves, at least at first, as North and South, but in the process of working together, evolved a more dynamic and fluid understanding of the politics of gender and poverty, to the point of questioning the original identification as Northern and Southern.

We describe the focus on gender and poverty of the Northern-based Network Women in Development Europe (WIDE) — a network of Northern women working in development and gender based largely in European NGOs — and the Southern based DAWN — an international group of women researchers and activists living and working in the South taking their cue from grassroots women's groups.

What follows here describes the discussions of the last decade between these groups of women in the 'North' and 'South' and how over these years, international development organisations and the women's

movement have shifted their perspectives on poverty. In telling this tale we show how Northern and Southern women have come to share their analysis of economics and politics, and are working on strategies to challenge inequality and poverty in all countries, rather than seeing them as phenomena belonging only to the South. Such alliances tackle women's particular experience of poverty based on gender inequality in ways that move beyond the concept of North or South.

Moving away from a WID approach

In the 1980s, women working in development co-operation, largely in institutions based or funded in the North, saw poverty as a chronic problem experienced most acutely by women in the South. The best way to 'alleviate' or 'eradicate' poverty was

Discussion at the UN Women's Conference, Beijing, 1995. UN Conferences have provided a valuable opportunity for women from the North and the South to meet and discuss shared concerns.

Nancy Durrell McKenna/Oxfam

to assist women's groups in the South by providing information, knowledge, and access to economic and technical resources. Northern women brought back observations gained from the 'field' to academic, policy-oriented or solidarity-based fora. Based on these observations, the Women in Development (WID) and Gender and Development (GAD) approaches evolved (WIDE *Bulletins* 1991–3, *Development* 1995.1; Kabeer 1995).

International development agencies sent Northern, and some Southern, professionals to visit communities in need in Southern countries. Their aim was invariably to work with women's groups to assist members to become involved in development projects and programmes which promoted various goals. Some were concerned with the 'empowerment' of women, while others merely attempted to alleviate women's disproportionately heavy workload. Typical project focuses were family planning, health, education, literacy, credit, and water supply and forestry schemes.

An alternative vision to WID

By the end of the 1980s there was a strong rejection of the idea of poor women as objects who needed to be observed and then 'assisted', while the complex, interlinked factors which were causing their poverty were ignored. With a growing sense of unease, women living in the North began to question their own role and the whole development process. They were worried that WID took an instrumental, piecemeal approach, and failed to take on board much larger issues which were much more difficult to change (WIDE *Bulletins* 1991–3).

They joined with Southern feminists who were highly critical of the WID approach for its failure to question fundamentally the nature of development or the unequal power balance between women and men. Groups of women from the South, including Development Alternatives with Women for a New Era (DAWN), which was founded in 1984, developed a complex analysis of poverty which stresses that, throughout the world, women experience poverty differently from the men in their group, since gender inequality mediates the effects of economic structural adjustment, crises in the global economy and the environment, the growing power of transnational companies, the domination of the market, the weakening of the state, civil unrest, and demand for greater democracy (ibid., *DAWN Informs*, 1992).

Redefining gender and poverty

From these critiques emerged a more dynamic understanding of gender and poverty based on the experience of Southern women living in poverty (DAWN 1996). The main elements of this new understanding are outlined below.

Defining poverty as more than economic

Being economically poor does not automatically mean being socially and culturally deprived; it cannot be assumed that communities who are identified as 'poor' want to change their situation by adopting different customs, and taking up new forms of employment and ways of living. Nor does it make sense to see women's experience of poverty as only affected by their gender identity. Women hold other aspects of social differentiation, such as disability or ethnicity, in common with the men in their community. Thus, their experience of poverty, and views on how to end it, may be similar in many respects, to those of men.

Gender and other aspects of identity

Other aspects of identity, including race, ethnicity, and class, have to be recognised as cross-cutting gender identity. An understanding of identity as made up of many, interlinked aspects should be part of the much larger project of questioning the concept of 'development' and North–South relations.

Rejecting images of passivity

This dynamic, highly critical approach to development has been particularly concerned about the labelling of women as marginalised victims. It was clear to women in both the South and North that development concerns the whole of people's lives, and cannot be conceptualised in terms of projects and programmes. The DAWN analysis and others see development as having been dominated by male ways of thinking, short-term trends, narrow sectoral foci, and racist attitudes which conceptualise Southern communities as full of grateful, passive recipients of aid who need to be 'taught'. The agendas of those involved in development, including government bodies and NGOs, are far from altruistic; the gains to the North from involvement in 'development' remain largely unacknowledged and unspoken.

Forming alliances North and South

A new dialogue between women from the North and the South evolved in the 1990s, facilitated by the opportunities for meeting provided by the UN Conferences of that decade. The challenge to the idea and practice of 'development' in the South — both the WID approach, and the subsequent failure of the GAD approach to address issues of power — meant that women from North and South had found some common ground. Northern women had begun to revise their position on gender and poverty, adopting 'Southern lenses' (Jain, quoted in WIDE *Bulletin* 1991). Southern women had started to look, if warily, at how to work strategically in partnership with women in the North, to challenge and change the global development structure which was impoverishing women, not only in the South, but worldwide (Oxfam UK/I Women's Linking Project; WIDE July 1995).

The 'lost decade'

The late 1980s to early 1990s was a period of uncertainty in international relations. The crisis of development was precipitated by the fall of the Berlin Wall, the understanding of the 1980s as a 'lost decade' for development (*Development* 1989), the decline of the power of individual states, and the floundering of the UN in its uncertain role in a changing world. Women development activists found themselves taking on issues of global importance: 'cleaning up the mess' as one put it (Peggy Antrobus, quoted in WIDE 1991).

Women working in networks of women's and feminist organisations, including Alternative Women in Development (Alt-WID) in the USA and Network Women in Development Europe (WIDE), built on the global analysis of poverty started in the 1980s by drawing parallels between the experiences of women in the South, and women living in poverty in the North (WIDE *Bulletin* 1991–3).

Our own experiences

An example of this shift in perception, and the implications that it has had for the international women's movement, can be seen in the series of dialogues between WIDE, DAWN, and the Society of International Development (SID), from 1989–1991. We, the authors of this article — Fatma Alloo as part of the African network of DAWN, and Wendy Harcourt through her work with WIDE and SID — met in this turbulent period, when Southern women were strongly challenging the position of Northern women in the 'development' of the South, and Northern women were trying to find their place in, and respond to, the analysis coming from Southern women. In discussions we attended, heated debates, both public and private, occurred, as each side defended its position, and gradually learned not to take sides, but to adjust to the other's perception.

The need for 'development' work in the North

Some high points (WIDE 1991–2) that we remember were a DAWN General Assembly in 1989, where Northern participants found themselves on the outside of the discussion about how to tackle regional approaches to development, gender, and poverty; and divided among themselves on the position they could take. Some opted for a professional development stance: that they were WID experts in certain regions, and therefore had the right to join their Southern colleagues working in the same regions. Others made the point that good feminist practice in development politics should begin at home, and therefore Northern practitioners should focus on work in their own regions. A major discussion among members of the WIDE network took place, resulting in a revision of WIDE's strategies of how it could contribute to the debates on gender and poverty. DAWN decided not to include Northern women in their General Assemblies in future.

Recognising the 'South in the North'

Another significant moment came at a WIDE/SID Assembly in 1990, where women from the 'South in the North' challenged their apparent exclusion from the analysis and work of WIDE. These participants had formed migrant women's groups, which were struggling for recognition, although, at the same time, WIDE was asserting the importance of 'Southern' views and analysis! This led WIDE to review its definitions of North and South, and the position of its Northern members on how 'gender and development' work, associated with developing countries, linked to work to combat the poverty of immigrant Southern women 'at home'. In 1991, there was a WIDE meeting in Dublin where indigenous women from North America were invited to talk about environmental issues. At that meeting, the case of the Irish tinkers[1] was presented as an experience of development gone wrong.

Building alliances for joint work

Through such debates, people shifted their positions; what had formerly been seen as two strands of thinking labelled 'Southern' and 'Northern' began to interweave, forming a solid feminist critique of social policy and development practice: a model of alternative development. In the process of debating these wide-ranging, diverse issues — at times quite hotly — women have determined at what level they can build alliances for joint work, including collaboration over publications, policy statements, lobbying efforts, and meetings.

These shared activities continued during the United Nations meetings focusing on women's rights, starting from the Earth Summit in Rio, Brazil, in 1992, and ending with the Fourth UN Women's Conference at Beijing, China, in 1995.

Our personal perspectives

The authors have witnessed this shift in thinking, and in terminology, from 'South' and 'North' to a mutually-owned international perspective, which gives a more holistic understanding of poverty and gender identity among women living in countries in varying stages of industrialisation. The next two sections of this article are our personal perspectives.

A view from the South: Fatma Alloo

The tool women journalists like me have in our hands is our pen; through it we can have an impact within the media. But in order to achieve an impact not only do we need to use the pen as a tool, but to organise as a group and become part of the women's movement. Time and effort was spent in confronting negative images of women, and portraying our own strong self-images. We had an impact on society through our coverage of issues like violence against women, reproductive rights, maternity leave, and training for women, and our ability to report on challenging stories.

As this strategy developed, so did our views on wider development issues: the connection between the macro- and micro-levels of development, and the impact of the macro-level on our part of the 'South'. For us, conceptualising men as the enemy was inconceivable; the central issue for us was poverty, and both men and women experienced it. Within that broad context, a major issue was the way our society has been made marginal to world development; and the issue within our own society which is most important was violation of women's rights as human beings.

Thus began our engagement with the international women's movement. We joined it at a high point in the early 1990s when many UN Conventions affecting women[2] were being passed, and we quickly became enmeshed in it. But the question we continued to ask was, 'what is our identity? where are we located in these debates?'

The more we experienced the North, the more we began to see — literally — the South in the North, in the form of poverty. The more we saw the South in the North, the more we began to be impatient with feminists from the North who saw poverty only as a problem which exists 'out there'; who kept telling us, 'we are here to help'! We began to understand that the North needs help itself. Within Tanzania Media Women's Association (TAMWA), we used to take volunteer workers from the North in the belief that professionals from the 'developed world' knew more than us and could teach us. But we eventually realised that unless Northern feminist volunteers came with experience of their own struggles, through belonging to a group or an NGO which works on women's issues at home, they had little to offer in our own context.

A new kind of relationship began to emerge after that realisation; one of partnership and solidarity between us and our colleagues from the North. Confrontation gave way to positive interactions, and an understanding that there is a real force for change at the moment, which comes from an alliance between the South of the North and the South of the South: women living in poverty in both contexts. For me, development is ultimately a class issue, because it is based on an awareness of poverty and a commitment to fighting it.

We realised that to understand and confront poverty throughout the world, we needed to confront the consumption patterns of the North. For example, the issues of environmental degradation, and sustainable development, must be seen as dependent on consumption patterns in industrialised countries; the blame for environmental degradation cannot be placed simply on women of the Third World cutting trees for firewood. Earning legitimacy on development issues does not result from women from 'developed' countries going to work and conduct research in the 'South'. It requires working in, and understanding, our own situation, wherever in the world we live, and using this experience to understand development patterns imposed on the South.

For women from Southern countries, a parallel understanding is needed: that not everyone in the 'North' is wealthy, and that women and men living in poverty in the North are marginalised. To understand the reasons behind the similar experiences of poor women throughout the world, we have to understand economic globalisation and the associated social and political changes.

A networking style began to emerge, involving the formation of deep bonds between those in the North who were willing to take on the issues, including WIDE, and those in the South, like DAWN and TAMWA. The Beijing conference and NGO forum in 1995 demonstrated the importance of such a partnership.

Perspectives from the North: Wendy Harcourt

In 1990 I was working with WIDE and the Society for International Development SID-

WID programme. I recall my discomfort, and that of other Northern feminists working on gender and poverty in development, with our role as WID or GAD 'experts'. We began at that time to define our political vision as women living in Europe, and from there defined how to engage more appropriately with Southern women's groups. The phrase then, coined by Devaki Jain from the DAWN network in 1991, in an open letter to European women's groups, was to put on 'Southern lenses', in order to analyse how gender and poverty issues in the North were linked to the development patterns imposed on the South (WIDE *Bulletin* 1991).

In understanding women's experience of living in poverty in the North in a more complex and holistic way, we found ourselves redefining poverty and its links to development patterns imposed on the South, and resisting the 'blame the victim' view of poverty which we often encounter in our societies. To arrive at a meeting of minds, we all needed to understand poverty worldwide as embedded in an inequitable and unjust system, which must be tackled with both a local and global analysis, regardless of our country context. In this analysis we acknowledged power relations based on differences of geography, history, race, ethnicity, and age.

This process of dialogue to find a shared analysis sometimes faltered, and some women were unconvinced. Some of these were WID 'experts' from 'developed' countries, who felt that they had a professional perspective which should not be belittled.

In 1993–4, WIDE undertook a study of women living in poverty in different countries in Europe, looking at the reasons for poverty and how women were facing it (WIDE July 1995). In these studies, a new concept of poverty was defined. The study looked at the changes in family structure; the growing numbers of single mothers; the hidden poverty of women as they are not represented in statistics and are beyond the reach of government services; the impact of the decline of the welfare state on education and health services as women have to take on more responsibility; the impact of environmental damage on family homes and quality of life; the growth of unemployment and industrial restructuring; the poverty linked to racism and ageism; and the strategies which women in solidarity with other women are adopting within their communities and through networks which support new forms of living and employment.

It was on the strength of this study, and the work done on globalisation, trade, and alternative economics from a European perspective, that WIDE broadened out its partnerships with women living and working in the South. (WIDE August 1995, WIDE March 1995, WIDE December 1996)

Looking back, this refocusing was heralded not only by the direct challenge by Southern groups such as DAWN and migrant women's groups to look at 'the South in the North'. It was also catalysed by the fear elicited by the shake-up in the world order caused by the fall of the Berlin Wall in 1989, and worry that the birth of the European Union in 1992 and the redrafting of social policy (including gender-related issues) would see a retraction of some progressive laws, (for example, legal entitlements to maternity leave) in some national states.

In addition, the spate of UN Conferences in the 1990s, beginning with the Earth Summit at Rio, Brazil, in 1992, allowed for large-scale networking and alliance-building with Southern women's groups as partners.

This refocusing was not easy, as it challenged our sense of identity, and the legitimacy of our previous work. It forced us to consider how to form alliances, not only with women in the South, but also with women and other activists in the North and, ultimately, to rewrite our own histories and agendas.

Fatma states that Southern women recognised that Northern women needed help themselves. I think this statement can be interpreted most usefully to mean not just the need to focus on the poverty occurring among women in the North which exists and is increasing, but also that women living in industrialised countries need to change their way of engaging in political struggle, to be far more conscious of the links among key development concerns, and the reasons for global environmental, social and economic breakdown.

To take up Fatma's point that redefining the environment and development debate meant rejecting the notion that it is a problem caused by the very poor in the South squandering the Earth's resources; it is a much graver problem, of the majority in industrialised countries who pursue an unsustainable way of life (Harcourt 1994). 'Environment' takes on a new meaning in this sense — it is no longer a separate entity where nature is divorced from human action, but a complex interactive system that is more difficult to understand than we had realised. In looking at the impact of environmental degradation on poor women living in the North, we recognised that they shared similar problems with women living in poverty in the South: lack of choice over habitat; lack of information on what was happening to their environment; lack of resources to change adverse conditions.

Taking a global perspective does not only emphasise the interlinkedness of the global economy in terms of our different positions within it. It also emphasises the similar concerns that affect populations worldwide. Another example was rural women in Europe — farmers in France, Switzerland and also the CEEC. Like women in the South facing the impact of industrialisation of agriculture, European women were facing the same problems of isolation, male migration, and loss of livelihoods upon the take-over of their farms by big industrial farming conglomerates, which turned the land over to mono-crop agriculture. We also began to be aware of the campaigns which European women's environmental groups were organising against over-packaging and pollution of rivers, including civil action on products such as nappies and sanitary napkins.

The Internet is one of the most powerful tools we have in helping us to learn about each other's contexts, and to work in solidarity in order to combat the growing impoverishment of women worldwide. Information, Communication and Technology (ICT) can change the nature of North–South relations and the methods that we have at our disposal to tackle gender and poverty. ICT offers a tool that women in an increasing number of countries can use; it can be a medium for political action, creating a powerful identity.

The Internet is a global network which is relatively cheap to use to effectively promote women's agendas and to confront and change other global agendas. The challenge is to enable all women to have access to and to become confident with the medium. Such a strategy will ensure that the growing and powerful global communication culture takes on a much more diverse perspective, responding and interacting to change the lives of poor and marginalised women in a positive way.

Fatma Alloo is currently Director of the NGO Resource Centre Zanzibar. She was founder and Director of TAMWA based in Dar es Salaam, and an active member of DAWN since its inception.

Wendy Harcourt is Director of Programmes for the Society for International Development, Rome, Italy, and Editor of Development. *Until 1995 she was on the Steering Group of WIDE and editor of the WIDE* Bulletin *and continues to support WIDE's work through membership of the Global Alliance for Alternative Development.*

Notes

1 Tinkers are travelling people who continue to live in caravans, supporting themselves by activities including selling goods and mending pots and pans.
2 Including Agenda 21 from the Earth Summit at Rio in 1992, the Vienna Declaration on Human Rights, and the Declaration from the Cairo Conference on Population and Development, 1994.

References

Braidotti, Rosi, Ewa Charkiewicz, Sabine Hausler and Saskia Wieringa (1994) *Women, The Environment and Sustainable Development*, London: ZED Books

DAWN (1992–4) *DAWN Informs*, WAND: Barbados.

Development (1989) 'Facing the Challenge: debt structural adjustment and world development', *Development Journal of the Society for International Development*, Rome: Italy.

Development (1995) 'Alternative Economics from a Gender Perspective', Guest Editor Peggy Antrobus, *Development Journal of the Society for International Development*, Rome: Italy

Harcourt, Wendy (ed) (1994) *Feminist Perspectives Towards Sustainable Development*, London ZED Books.

Kabeer, Naila, (1995) *Reversed Realities*, London: Verso.

WIDE (1991–3) *WIDE Bulletins*, Rome: Society for International Development.

WIDE (March 1995) 'Gender Mapping the European Union', Brussels.

WIDE (July 1995) 'Living and Working: an illustration of the feminisation of poverty in Europe', Brussels.

WIDE (August 1995) 'Towards Alternative Economics from a European Perspective', Brussels.

WIDE (December 1996) 'Women and Trade: European Strategies for an International Agenda', Brussels.

Gender, race, and the 'underclass':
the truth behind the American Dream

Sara Chamberlain

Although the economy is booming, America has the highest poverty levels in the industrialised world. This article looks at the way in which welfare policies are influenced by attitudes to poverty and to poor people, and argues for a different approach based on an accurate analysis of the causes of poverty.

According to most economic indicators, America is in great shape. It has the most powerful economy in the world, less than 5.5 per cent unemployment, and negligible inflation. The stock market has increased by 30 per cent in the last 12 months alone, and corporate profitability has reached post-war records. Yet 13.7 per cent of the population, some 36.5 million people, live below the official poverty line (US Census Bureau, 1997).

If the economy is doing so well, why are so many Americans poor? Politicians, academics, policy makers, and charitable organisations in America have debated this question since the 1800s. In general, explanations fall into two categories: those that blame the welfare state and the poor themselves, and those that place responsibility on economic factors.

Defining poverty

Americans are defined as 'poor' if their incomes fall below an official 'poverty line'. The official poverty line was established in 1963 by the United States Department of Agriculture (USDA), and is based on the assumption that food expenditure constitutes 33 per cent of a family's budget (University of Wisconsin 1995). The official poverty level is calculated on the cost of a minimum diet, multiplied by three to allow for shelter, clothing and other basic necessities. In 1996, the poverty level was $7,795 for one; $10,233 for a family of two; $12,516 for a family of three; and $16,036 for a family of four (US Census Bureau, 1997).

Most Americans, according to the influential Gallup Poll, think the official poverty level income is grossly inadequate. Gallup Poll respondents estimated that a family of four would need 140–160 per cent of the official poverty level income to meet their basic needs (ibid). While these figures may seem high compared to poverty lines in Southern contexts, poverty in America is real: 20–30 million Americans regularly do not have enough to eat. As a result, many means-tested federal poverty assistance programmes, such as food stamps, do not use the official poverty line to determine eligibility for benefits (University of Wisconsin, 1995).

Since 1963, the official poverty threshold has only been updated for price changes. It has thus failed to take into account changes in expenditure patterns, brought on, for example, by dramatic rent increases since the 1960s. It also fails to take into account income and social security taxes, and additional expenses relating to child care, health, and work. According to a panel established by the Committee on National Statistics of the National Research Council, in response to a request by the US Congress, 7.4 million 'new' people would slip beneath the official poverty line if these expenses and taxes were taken into account.[1] Almost half these 'new' poor — or 3.6 million people — would live in families where the primary earner worked at least 48 hours a week (University of Wisconsin 1995).

Popular explanations for poverty in America

Policy responses to poverty alleviation in America are influenced by the ideology underlying explanations for the existence of poverty.

The American Dream and the Protestant work ethic

Many Americans still believe that if they work hard, they will succeed against all odds. Despite the fact that 31.2 per cent of the American workforce earns wages that keep it in poverty (Burtless and Mishel 1995) (an increase of almost 10 per cent on 1973 levels), and that 56 per cent of poor Americans live in working-poor households (ibid), many Americans think poverty is the result of a diminished work ethic. The roots of this misconception lie in the myth of the 'American Dream' (Danziger and Gottschalk, 1995). The American Dream promises them that if they strive in the land of opportunity, they are guaranteed a higher standard of living

than their parents. This myth fosters the view that those who remain poor must be personally responsible for their misfortune. 'One of the defining characteristics of American society, which makes it unique among other Western societies is the emphasis — indeed, the reverence for — work' (Duerr Berrick, 1995).

The idea that women and men living in poverty have a diminished work ethic is useful in allowing many more affluent Americans to abdicate responsibility for inequality in society. Poverty is blamed on the behaviour, attitudes, and values of the poor, which create a self-perpetuating 'culture of poverty', setting women, men, and their children apart from mainstream society, preventing them from becoming successful Americans.'

Culture of poverty and the evolution of the welfare state

'Culture of poverty' theories have persisted in America since the late nineteenth century, when Francis Walker, the head of the US Census in 1897, concluded that 'pauperism is largely voluntary... Those who are paupers are so far more from character than from condition. They have the pauper trait; they bear the pauper brand' (quoted in Patterson, 1995, 21). Attitudes like this had a profound effect on poverty-alleviation policy. In the 1880s and 1890s, charities and social workers made efforts to abolish all so-called 'hand-outs' to the poor, arguing that they damaged the work ethic, and recommending 'preventative measures' including teaching the poor the 'virtues of self-discipline and the joys of work in poor-houses and orphanages' (ibid, 24).

The Depression of the 1930s challenged these attitudes insofar as consensus was achieved around the idea that there were 'truly deserving' poor, including the unemployed, who should receive public assistance. However, the idea of the 'dole' (money paid by the state to the unemployed) was still universally condemned. 'Work relief', where the government paid people to work for the state for minimal wages, was preferred, being seen as a way of preserving the work ethic while helping people in need. At its peak in February 1934, President Franklin D. Roosevelt's work-relief programme, and other relief programmes, directly involved 22.2 per cent per cent of the American population (ibid).

Just one year later, however, Roosevelt argued that 'continued dependence upon relief induces a spiritual and moral disintegration fundamentally destructive to the national fibre. To dole out relief in this way is to administer a narcotic, a subtle destroyer of the human spirit ... the government must and shall quit this business of relief' (quoted in ibid, 59). The responsibility of central government for 'general relief' was handed to the individual states.

Although the federal government retained financial responsibility for work relief, it only agreed to match funds raised by the states to pay for 'categorical assistance' to the blind, aged, and dependent children. It also asked the employed to contribute to a 'social security' fund that would help to support them if they became unemployed, and when they eventually retired (ibid). At the time, Aid to Dependent Children (ADC) — which has since become the largest and most important 'categorical assistance' programme — was mainly responsible for the children of divorced or deserted mothers. ADC was a source of contention even then, in the aftermath of the Depression. Like its critics in the 1980s, conservatives in the late 1930s thought ADC 'encouraged family break ups, and that public money should not be poured into broken homes' (ibid, 68).

Race and poverty in America

'The only safe generalisation to make about the dependent poor', wrote a progressive American in the 1800s, 'is that they are poor ... The differentiating factors are economic rather than moral or religious, social rather than personal, accidental and remedial rather than functional' quoted in Patterson 1995, 22)

However, in popular mythology and the discourse of politicians, in the United States, racial identity and economic status are tightly intertwined (Newitz and Wray, 1997). The term 'white trash', used to make derogatory reference to poor, rural white Americans since the 1800s, is an expression of this perceived link. It is both a class term — used to distinguish so-called waste or garbage of society from the rich — and a term of racial abuse, distinguishing white people in poverty from other groups including Afro-Caribbeans, Hispanics, and Asians (Newitz and Wray 1997, 4).

'White trash' is used in 'racialised contexts where class and race differences become conflated, overlapping rather than remaining clear and distinct' (John Hartigan Junior, 1997, 47). The term was invented by black slaves to refer to poor whites. Prior to slavery, poor white Americans worked on the vast plantations of the South. Slavery displaced them, forcing them off the land and into poverty. Black slaves used the term 'white trash' to distinguish between these poor whites and the affluent plantation owners (ibid).

Despite the fact that the term 'white trash' originated in a situation of genuine economic hardship and deprivation, it became synonymous with 'poor, drunken, criminally minded, sexually perverse people' who were considered the 'dregs of society' (ibid., 4), and the 'riff-raff of colonialism' (Dunbar 1997, 76). The term was popularised by eugenicists of the late 1800s and early 1900s, who set out to 'demonstrate scientifically that large numbers of rural poor whites were "genetic defectives"' (Newitz and Wray 1997, 2). The tracing of criminals' genealogies back to supposedly defective sources by the US

Eugenics Records Office resulted in the involuntary sterilisation of large numbers of rural poor whites in the early years of the twentieth century (ibid).

Newitz and Wray think Americans find the term 'white trash' useful, because 'in a country so steeped in the myth of class-lessness, where we are often at a loss to explain or understand poverty, the white trash stereotype serves as a useful way of blaming the poor for being poor' (ibid, 4).

Women, family values, and the 'underclass'

As the spectre of impoverished rural whites faded from the imaginations of middle-class Americans, a new scapegoat for poverty emerged. Again racialised and classed, this new scapegoat was young, urban and black. 'Poor and black are virtually synonymous in the American mind' (Henwood in Newitz and Wray, 1997, 177). But for conservative politicians and the public to dismiss poverty as a 'black problem', is to ignore the statistics. In 1993, almost half of those living below the official poverty line were non-Hispanic whites (ibid).

The mixed racial composition of the American poor is also ignored in popular stereotyping of the 'underclass' because this tends to focus on the perceived behaviour of the poor, rather than on their numbers or identities. The issue at stake is the perceived breakdown of American family values: the proliferation of single-parent families and illegitimate births, especially among African Americans in the inner-city slums, which threatens the moral fibre of the nation.

The myth of 'welfare mothers'

Conservative ideologues such as Charles Murry, whose book *Losing Ground* is credited with popularising the notion of an underclass, argue that state benefits such as AFDC encourage poor young women to

have children, so that they can live off the American taxpayer. Once on welfare, they are depicted as losing the ability to support themselves, or in the case of teenage mothers, as never having developed it in the first place. These women became addicted to benefits, just as they would to a drug. According to such theories, the underclass consists of dependent, lazy people with bad attitudes and messy family lives: 'demonising people who are poor allows us to step away and feel that somehow those who are poor are not quite like us' (Hayes Bautista, 1995).

In fact, there is very little evidence that there is such a connection between single-parent family forms and welfare. Even though the percentage of children living in single-parent families rose from 14 to 20 per cent during the 1960s, the number of children living in families collecting AFDC remained constant at about 12 per cent. In other words, the trend towards single-parent families seems to have been less evident among people collecting AFDC than the nation as a whole. In addition, there was no motive to remain single in order to collect AFDC after 1961, when the benefit had been extended to cover two-parent families. Furthermore, the number of African American children in welfare families actually decreased by 5 per cent during this period, discounting the theory that African American women are particularly susceptible to the lures of welfare (Duerr Berrick, 1995).

Secondly, there is no evidence that AFDC payments encourage young women to keep having children so that they can stay on the welfare rolls. According to Jill Duerr Berrick, author of *Faces of Poverty: Portraits of Women and Children on Welfare*, 'a growing body of evidence suggests that women on welfare are less likely to have an additional child than women who are not on AFDC (Duerr Berrick 1995, 15). In fact, Duerr Berrick says that 'recent studies have found that women on welfare are more conscientious about using contraceptives' (ibid, 15). Raising even one child on welfare is challenging.

Family budgeting on welfare

Kathryn J. Edin, an Assistant Professor at Rutgers University, states that 'in no state do welfare payments lift a family above the poverty line, and one half of AFDC recipients have incomes well below half the poverty standard' (Edin, 1995). Benefit levels, when adjusted for inflation, have fallen by 43 per cent since 1970. As always, welfare cuts have been fuelled by stereotypes of lazy, good-for-nothing recipients, who sign on because they simply do not want to work. For example, in 1992, California's governor, Pete Wilson, proposed a 25 per cent cut in AFDC benefits, arguing that welfare recipients would simply have less money 'for a six pack of beer' (quoted in Duerr Berrick 1995, 9). It is ironic that two-thirds of welfare recipients are children, who cannot legally work, let alone drink!

Because welfare payments are so low in most states (as little as $120 per month for a family of three in the state of Mississippi in 1994) (Edin 1995), many recipients are forced to supplement their incomes with unreported work (ibid). Of the mothers on welfare interviewed in a recent study, 46 per cent supplemented their welfare checks with unreported earnings (ibid). Reporting earnings is not possible since benefits would be correspondingly reduced. This statistic of participation in waged work directly contradicts the popular stereotype of the lazy welfare mother; in fact, it is more common to find 'welfare mothers' working long and hard to survive, including making every effort to find work, so that they can escape the humiliation of being dependent on the state. As Sheldon Danziger writes in *America Unequal*, 'if welfare were addictive, we would expect a larger fraction of those who get benefits to stay on the rolls as long as they legally can. This is not the case at all. Most people who go on welfare get off in less than two years'. In fact 89 per cent of all welfare recipients leave the rolls before they become ineligible (Danziger 1995, 71).

The economics of poverty

The alternative to welfare is low pay and long hours, with little or no opportunity to obtain good care for children and other dependents. Despite brisk economic growth, the last 20 years have been characterised by widespread wage deterioration and growing income inequality. According to the US Census Bureau, income inequality increased by 22.2 per cent between 1968 and 1992 (Weinberg 1997). Between 1992 and 1994 alone, the median wage fell 3.3 per cent, and median family income sunk 6.6 per cent below its 1989 level. The median wage has continued to decline since 1995. It is now 4.6 per cent below its 1989 level (Teixeira and Rogers, 1996).

Declining wages and falling incomes in recent years have been responsible for a massive increase in the working poor. In 1992, 18 per cent of full-time workers (14 per cent of men and 24 per cent of women workers) earned less than the official poverty level income for a family of four. For example, in 1993 an American employed full-time at the minimum wage could expect to earn $8,500 a year (Patterson, 1995, 230). This was a little above the poverty line for a single person, below the line for a couple, and completely inadequate for a family with only one wage-earner. The largest growth has been among workers earning very low wages, or less than 75 per cent of the poverty level income (Burtless and Mishel 1995). In 1979, poor people who worked for very low wages comprised 4.1 per cent of the working population; in 1989 they were 13.2 per cent (ibid).[2]

Race and gender identities interact to affect the likelihood of individuals being in very poorly paid work. Although women are much more likely to earn poverty-level wages than men, the largest growth in low-wage work has occurred among men from ethnic minorities. In 1979, 25.1 per cent of black men earned poverty-level wages, while in 1991, 38.6 per cent earned poverty wages, with most of the increase being in the number earning very low wages; however, ethnic minority women are still more likely than ethnic minority men to earn low-level wages (ibid).

Between 1981 and 1990 the minimum wage remained static, while its value, when adjusted for inflation, declined a great deal. For example in 1993, the value of the minimum was over $1.3 less, in inflation-adjusted terms, than it was in 1979 (Burtless and Mishel 1995). The globalisation of capital and manufacturing has reduced the power of the unions, which has meant that there has been little pressure from them to raise the minimum wage. Weak collective bargaining power has also meant a reduction in work-related benefits, such as health and child care, which has forced many Americans on to welfare (Duerr Berrick, 1995).

Finally, some researchers link the introduction of new production techniques, and technological change in both the goods-producing and service-producing industries to rising unemployment among the most disadvantaged section of American society (Burtless and Mishel, 1995). For example, technological change has reduced the demand for low-skilled workers, and increased the demand for high-skilled workers, which has led to increased competition and unemployment among the low-skilled. It is this variety of facts and statistics, not lax attitudes towards work, that have forced one in ten Americans to collect food stamps and 13 million Americans on to welfare.

Family stereotypes and economic reality

Many liberal academics and policy makers blame reduced wages and employment opportunities for low-skilled workers for changes in family form, or the so-called decline in 'family values'. Eleanor Holmes Norton, an African American Chairwoman of the Equal Opportunities Commission during the 1980s, believes that women have little incentive to marry if their prospective husbands are unemployed and destitute, while men who lack job prospects are in no position to take on the financial responsibilities of a family (quoted in Patterson 1994, 220). Thus, marriage rates have declined among those most affected by the current economic climate.

As Jill Duerr Berrick observes, in *Faces of Poverty: Portraits of Women and Children on Welfare*, 'as long as children are growing up in poverty, where they are reminded each day that they have little to look forward to, some girls will continue to choose early pregnancy and parenthood. In a world that regularly denies these girls participation in the mainstream and in which the system itself is not concerned about how they turn out, a baby is regarded as an opportunity for self expression' (Duerr Berrick 1995, 160). In other words, if you have little chance of finding fulfilling employment, and have never had much of anything to call your own, a baby may seem your only hope for achievement and happiness.

Policy implications

If popular explanations of poverty dismiss millions of Americans as an 'underclass', beyond hope, then surely it is time for new concepts, informed by the realities of American poverty, to be developed. It would appear that American women and men living in poverty are a racially and socially diverse population of busy, industrious people, working hard to make ends meet and bring up children in a hostile economic environment. The American Dream has failed them; instead, they are faced with a choice between poverty-level wages with no benefits, or a meagre welfare payment and illegal work.

Because the American poor are so diverse, with such different needs and capabilities, blanket policies are inappropriate. Policies that might help single mothers would not be suitable for factory workers facing redundancy, or mentally ill people who are not offered the support networks they need to live independently. And within each of these categories, many variations exist. Mothers on welfare are not all the same; their job skills, levels of training, and responsibilities to their families vary dramatically. 'If women on welfare have diverse needs, policies and programmes should provide diverse services' (Duerr Berrick 1995, 147).

Yet despite their diversity, two valid generalisations can be made about the American poor: the majority of them are women and children; and they are all hurt by declining wages and reduced benefits. Taking this into consideration, several changes could be made to the existing welfare system that would greatly benefit women and children. Firstly, the duration of free child-care benefits should be extended. Transitional child-care (TCC) benefits, which were recently added to the AFDC package when policy makers recognised that prohibitively high child-care costs prevented single mothers from working, are available to all women on welfare who sign up to the JOBS programme.[3] However, TCC is only available to women who leave welfare for work completely, and then only for a one-year period. Jill Deurr Berrick points out that this restriction is not realistic, because few women find jobs that pay enough to get them completely off welfare. Instead, most women who work part-time continue receiving a reduced AFDC payment (ibid). In addition, cutting child care off completely after one year is not 'transitional'. It would be far more useful if child-care benefits were gradually reduced as a woman's earnings increased, until she was making enough money to pay for child care herself.

Welfare mothers would also be greatly helped if they were allowed to work without having their benefits correspond-ingly reduced. The current system makes liars of welfare recipients who must work to cover their costs. This change would also help to dispel the misconceptions that welfare mothers are lazy and addicted to benefits.

The quality of life of many poor Americans would also be improved if health care were extended to cover all poor Americans, not just welfare recipients. One of the main reasons why single mothers go on welfare is because few low-wage jobs offer health-care benefits. Between 1989 and 1992 the number of Americans without health care for some period of time increased by 4.2 million, to 38.9 million. Aside from South Africa, America is the only industrialised nation without a comprehensive, publicly managed national health system (Patterson, 1995, 231). It has been estimated that the welfare caseload would drop by 16 per cent if all working women had health coverage (Duerr Berrick, 1995, 44).

Although extending child care and health care, and allowing welfare recipients to supplement their welfare checks with earnings, would definitely ease the suffering of many poor families, these will continue to be stop-gap measures only, as long as wages for women continue to decline. 'Any set of reforms that fails to recognise the fundamental inadequacy of low-wage jobs will simply add further instability to the already precarious situation of many poor families' (Edin 1995, 11). Women will have no incentive to leave welfare if the jobs they can get are not adequately paid. The Jobs Opportunities and Basic Skills programme (JOBS), introduced by several state governments in 1988, was intended to increase the work potential of welfare recipients. But it failed because it tended to place recipients in low-wage jobs in the service sector.

The current welfare system is imperfect at best. It does not lift women and children out of poverty. It forces women to lie about their incomes, and does not offer them the child care and job training they need to help themselves. To quote Jill Duerr Berrick:

'Welfare will never be removed from the public agenda as long as we continue to tinker with it only at the edges and ignore the real issues of inadequate job prospects, poor education, low wages, and all of poverty's attendant problems' (Duerr Berrick 1995, 51).

Sara Chamberlain is the editor of Oxfam UK and Ireland's Web site, and an assistant editor of New Internationalist *magazine.*
Contact: schamberlain@oxfam.org.uk

Notes

1   Conversely, if state benefits including food stamps, public housing, Medicair and welfare were counted as income, 7.4 million people would rise above the poverty line (University of Wisconsin, 1995).

2   An in-depth explanation of the factors that have contributed to wage deterioration and increasing inequality in America is beyond the scope of this article. Suffice to say that macro-economic trends, such as the migration of manufacturing jobs abroad, have left large numbers of displaced factory workers competing for employment in the service sector. As a result of increased competition, service-sector wages have dropped and the number of people earning poverty-level wages has risen (Burtless and Mishel, 1995).

3   The Jobs Opportunities and Basic Skills (JOBS) programme trains and places welfare recipients in jobs.

References

Burtless, G and Mishel, L (1995) *Recent Wage Trends: The Implications for Low-wage Workers*, London: Economic Policy Institute.

Danziger, S and Gottschalk, P (1995) *America Unequal*, New York: Russell Foundation and Harvard University Press..

Duerr Berrick, J (1995) *Faces of Poverty: Portraits of Women and Children on Welfare*, Oxford: Oxford University Press.

Edin, K J (1995)) *The Myths of Dependence and Self-sufficiency: Women, Welfare, and Low-waged Work*, University of Wisconsin.

Hayes Bautista, D (1995) 'Poverty and the underclass: some Latino Uundercurrents' in Danziger and Gottschalk.

John Hartigan Junior (1997), 'Name calling' in Newitz, A and Wray, M.

Henwood, D (1997) 'Trash-o-nomicks' , in Newitz, A and Wray, M.

Newitz, A and Wray, M (1997) *White Trash: Race and Class in America*, London:Routledge.

Patterson, J T (1995) *America's Struggle against Poverty 1900–94*, New York: Harvard University Press.

Texeira and Rogers, (1996) *Volatile Voters: Declining Living Standards and Non-college Educated Whites*, Economic Policy Institute.

University of Wisconsin (1995) 'Measuring poverty: a new approach' *Focus* 17:1, University of Wisconsin.

Power and dignity:
women, poverty, and Credit Unions

Annette Rimmer

This article looks at poverty amongst black and white women in Britain, and proposes that Credit Unions (community banks) could lead the way in establishing a feminist anti-poverty strategy offering not only financial but also socio-political and emotional benefits.

No apologies are made for the seemingly over-dramatic title of the article: it is intended to reflect the increase in power and confidence that I witnessed in the women with whom I worked in a community Credit Union. As someone with experience of community and social work in a variety of settings since the 1970's, my discovery of the Credit Union movement gave me hope and inspiration. At last, an organisation which extols women's strengths instead of exploiting them. At last 'a bank with a heart' (Doherty 1981). Little has been written about the 'many social and political advantages and the major steps in personal development gained from Credit Union membership' (Berthoud and Hinton p.89) and even less about the particular advantages for oppressed groups including women.

The research

Poverty is not only about shortage of money. It is about rights and relationships; about how people are treated and how they regard themselves; about powerlessness, exclusion and loss of dignity. Yet the lack of adequate income is at its heart (Archbishop of Canterbury's Commission on Urban Priority Areas, quoted in Harker and Oppenheim 1996, p7).

The article draws on a participatory research project, initiated in 1989, with a group of black and white women living in an area of Britain considered to be among the poorest 2 per cent of urban areas in Western Europe. In order to preserve confidentiality, the inner-city community which was the focus of my study will be referred to as Santon. The area was characterised by boarded-up shopping precincts, high-rise council flats, and a high incidence of reported crime. The majority of the population were members of families headed by lone mothers. The local bank and many shops had closed, and the only booming business seemed to be money-lending.

The aims of the project were to raise awareness in the area about Credit Unions, and to increase the power of women in the existing Santon Credit Union. This Community Credit Union, administered from a local Community Centre, had around 200 members who lived or worked in Santon. The majority of members were women, but the chair, vice-chair, treasurer and most officers of the Credit Union were white men.

I initiated the project by making contact with a small group of African Caribbean women already using the Community Centre, and through their networking skills, the group grew quickly. I worked closely with this group for a year, and the practical aims were decided upon by consensus. The group also knew from the start that I would be writing about it, and about the experience of individual members, as part of my MA research.

The research was not intended as a dispassionate, impartial enquiry, but one seeking to influence change. 'To talk of a feminist methodology is clearly political, controversial and implies personal and/ or political sympathies on the part of the researcher' (Donnelly 1986, p3). The project methodology was based upon the principle that feminist, qualitative enquiry seeks to give voice to people 'whose everyday histories ... have been condemned to silence' (McRobbie 1982, p46).

Poverty in Britain

The principle underpinning my study is that poverty exists in Britain, 'blight[ing] the lives of around a quarter of the UK population, and a third of its children' (Child Poverty Action Group, 1993). The European Decency Threshold (poverty line) for a co-habiting man, woman and two children is £166 per week, yet the social security benefit for a family is £115 (Harker and Oppenheim 1996).

From 1979 to 1997, 18 years of Conservative government in the UK saw 'a growth in unemployment, a fall in wage rates and reductions in the scope and level of welfare benefits' (Kempson 1996; Pascall 1986). Some respondents did not claim income support; they were employed, yet received less than they would have done had they claimed benefit.

In comparison to definitions of absolute poverty with respect to the Majority World (otherwise known as the South, or 'less-developed world'), where women and men experience devastating and life-threatening poverty, poverty in Britain needs to be defined in relative terms: 'it is not sufficient to assess poverty by absolute standards; nowadays it must be judged on relative criteria by comparison with the standard of living of other groups in the community... beneficiaries must have an income which enables them to participate in the life of the community' (Harker and Oppenheim 1996, p10). Poverty in the UK is experienced disproportionately by women: in Britain today 59 per cent of adults supported by income support (government social security) are women (ibid)

Reduced self-esteem and poor mental health

Economic poverty is linked to social and political marginalisation, which has effects on physical and mental health. Brady, in *Living in Debt*, talks of women having the main burden of family debts, and reported that they felt depressed, worried and anxious, suffered from sleepless nights, increased dependency on alcohol and antidepressant drugs, thoughts of suicide, and suicide attempts (Brady, 1984). Mind, the British mental health charity, supported these claims during its 'Stress on Women' Campaign in 1992: '46 million prescriptions of anti-depressants, two-thirds of these going to women each year' (Mind, 1992).

In line with this, participants in the research project confirmed that there is a close link between poverty, humiliation and depression:

I remember once going to this birthday dinner which said 'food provided' but it wasn't. Everybody ordered a hot cooked meal and I only had £1. I remember somebody left a roast potato and I was dying to eat it. It was so humiliating.

I get the bus after 9.30am because the fare is cheaper. Some drivers kick you off even at 9.29am if you don't pay full. This happens to me all the time even though I've waited half an hour and I've only got 45p. The thing is, I can feel the whole queue staring at me and thinking 'another black trying to dodge her fare'. I feel so put down and I know he'd let me on if I was white.

Low self-esteem in relationships with men

Lack of self-esteem in marital relationships was common among the women. Typical comments included:

I feel like crying, and I don't want to talk to no-one. I can't stop in the house when me and him argue. I don't want to make love or want him to touch me. Last time he hit me and said, 'you don't keep the house clean, you slut'. He never says anything good. I starting knitting him a jumper, and he says 'you'll never finish that', or 'it'll look stupid'. I feel useless at everything ... then he says, 'go out and make friends', and I did at the nursery and the Credit Union, so he says, 'you're always out, you slag... you never stay in'. Last time I treated myself was about a year ago, to new shoes which cost £1.99, and a dress for £4.99. He said 'no wonder the money's gone down!'

Many's the time I say to my friend, 'I'm gonna top myself' [commit suicide] and she says to me, 'don't be so stupid, what about your kids?' I say, 'well, somebody else can look after them', and she'll go, 'well, you surely don't want his other women to look after them', and I say, 'you gotta be joking'.

He don't take me places because I've got too many grey hairs, and he says I'm too fat. He likes girls with lighter skin.

I hear so many rumours about him having kids with other women. I was told he was shopping in Asda with another woman. That hurt because here I am with his four children and he hasn't been shopping with me for seven years. That makes me feel like shit.

Gender-differentiated spending patterns

The research also highlighted gender differences in attitudes to money. When money is short, women and men have different spending priorities. Pahl illustrates vividly women's lack of economic strength within the family (Pahl 1989). Even when the male partner is earning a significant salary, this does not mean his income is fairly distributed. Even in better-off households, the woman may have little or no control over money and feel that she is poor.

He used to have stupid hobbies like photography and he'd buy all these bleeding expensive cameras and then he'd be into tropical fish — all things that cost loads of money. He couldn't just have a camera, he'd have to have long lenses and short lenses and all that. He always wanted the best even though we couldn't afford it and the kids needed things. I never even had a vacuum cleaner.

He was really bleeding tight. He always treated the kids and saw them alright but I would always be short and worried about the rent and bills. There was no logic in him, he'd take the kids down the road and buy toys when they needed clothes ... when I was with him I was always skint [had no money], then after I got divorced, I was bleeding loaded [rich]. For those years I never had to draw my family allowance. How many people can say that?

(It emerged that this respondent's income did not actually increase at all, but after her divorce, she became the breadwinner and had total control over the income, which was still low.)

Another less exposed dimension on women's poverty is the fact that respondents who called themselves 'lone mothers' actually had partners who occasionally lived with them for two or three days, eating their food, using fuel, and contributing erratically to the family income. Some women had state benefits stopped by social security fraud officers when this happened. Few existing texts comment on this ambiguity about the security or status of women's relationship with their sexual partners, which undoubtedly added to both the financial and emotional insecurity of the women I interviewed:

I never really know when he'll be stopping the night, but when he does come he expects his dinner on the table with the kids'.

The fact that poverty forces women to acquire skills in financial management was recognised by women involved in the project. One said: 'women have to be financial wizards ... they have to make a meal for five on £2 every day. They are the best accountants in the world.' The regional Financial Training Officer for Credit Unions who covered Santon stated:

The vast majority of my time is not spent teaching accounts and bookkeeping. It is spent trying to convince women they are capable of doing the work. They hear the word 'Treasurer', and they say 'I can't do that, I'm too thick'. I wish I had a pound for every time I've said 'you can do it, you've brought up three kids and run a household on income support'.

Financial services available to women in poverty

What ways are open to women living in poverty who seek a way out of the trap of economic and social marginalisation?

Money-lenders and 'loan sharks'
There is no legislation in Britain to prevent anyone becoming a money-lender, and no limits upon the amount of interest they can

charge on a loan. Some established 'reputable' companies attached to multi-national insurance companies, charge 50 per cent plus; whilst some 'loan sharks' charge up to 400 per cent and will resort to violence and theft in order to make their victims pay. Conventional banks generally charge around 20 per cent but most unwaged people in Britain have no bank account. People living on a low income have access only to high-interest credit such as those mentioned, or catalogue companies, and pawnbrokers (National Money Advice Centre, Birmingham 1989).

Conventional banking services
The organisational culture of banks is one which places profit before the welfare of their clients. One Resource Manager of a branch in the survey area stated: 'we closed the branch in Santon because it wasn't feasible. We are interested in people without a vast amount of money, but we are a business after all, and not social services.' In line with this, conventional banks ask for references, insist on a minimum deposit and generally require the prospective member to be waged. For many women and men in poverty, banks did not offer sufficient flexibility in saving to suit the small, erratic amounts that they were able to save:

Well, to be honest, I don't have enough money to put in the bank. I'm lucky if there's a quid [£1] left over, and it costs 60p to get to the bank and back, so what's the point?

They'd laugh at me because I only save £2.50 a week.

I can't remember the last time I didn't come out crying after visiting the Bank Manager.

Women need a banking system which responds to their daily lives and economic situations, which differ from those of men. Many women have caring responsibilities, and this constrains their opportunities

to travel outside the immediate neighbourhood:

*My branch closed down about six years ago, and
I'd have to go into town with a double buggy
[push-chair for two children]. It was too much
trouble.*

Our research project produced some
profound statements from women about the
androcentric culture of financial systems in
our society, for example:

*They told me I couldn't join because I had no job
and they asked what my husband did. I told them
I hadn't got one.*

Community saving and credit unions

A Credit Union, simply defined, is a financial co-operative, a group of people who are
joined together by a 'common bond', such as
living in a particular neighbourhood, and
who save and then borrow from the pooled
savings. The most basic function of the
Credit Union is obviously to provide low-
interest credit to people who have not
previously been able to obtain it.

Credit Unions seem to be part of a collective response, on the part of people living in
poverty, to draconian welfare policies and a
low-wage economy. Currently, in the USA,
54 million people belong to Credit Unions,
while in Canada one in four people belong
(Berthoud and Hinton 1989).[2]

It is stated widely on Credit Union
publicity that 'Credit Unions are not about
profit, but about people' (Berthoud and
Hinton 1989/National publicity literature).
Credit Unions emphasise that loans are
given according to the savings record of the
member. A member can save as little as 50p
per week, and can generally borrow double
or treble the amount saved, at a low rate of
interest. One participant stated:

*I got a loan of £200 from the loan company and
spent the year paying back £298. If I'd been in*

*the Credit Union last year I'd have only paid
back £213. I'll never go to the loan company again.*

'Credit Unions are one of the few financial
groupings that have thrived during UK
recession' (McKillop et al 1995, p48). In
Britain, growth took place particularly
during the 1980s, after an 'unprecedented
growth in the use of consumer credit and
the widening gap between rich and poor as
a result of high unemployment and growing
wage differentials' (ibid.).

In addition to the individual benefits
there are wider economic benefits to
disadvantaged communities; Credit Unions
can slow down economic decline by preventing 'income slippage': since more money
is in circulation in the community, the spiral
of decline in businesses serving the
community is slowed. Involvement in a
Credit Union can also increase awareness of
other co-operative groups providing a
service, for example, food co-operatives.

Involvement in a Credit Union can also
encourage involvement in other community
activities. During the project in Santon,
black women began to make greater use of
other community groups, including self-
defence classes, a food co-operative, and a
toy library, which had previously been used
predominantly by white women. The
women also organised presentations against
loan sharks, on local radio, and in other
community groups.

Women's access to the Credit Union

In the particular Credit Union in the area
studied, access issues were addressed
through cashiers visiting places where
women met, including nursery coffee-
mornings, keep-fit classes, bingo sessions,
and residential homes for older people.
Cashiers did business wherever women
were, collecting money and organising loan
applications during nursery coffee mornings

A Credit Union and Advice Centre, in Oxford.

with children playing all around, and visiting disabled women in their homes. The local bingo caller announced that cashiers were collecting that evening.

However, it was clear that further action was needed to free women to participate in the Credit Union. Facilities needed to be designed at local and national level which recognised the different claims on women's time. One woman stated that, in the absence of child-care facilities, she was being forced to consider leaving the Union.

Empowering effects of Credit Unions

In all UK and Ireland Credit Unions, women are the majority members (information from ABCUL and the Irish League of Credit Unions). Much has been written about the social, as well as economic, benefits of women joining together for support and collective action (Dominelli and McLeod 1989, Donnelly 1986). Yet little has so far been written about the non-financial benefits to women of involvement in Credit Unions. However, I would argue that such involvement can potentially restore the confidence

and dignity of women, and raise their economic and political consciousness whilst offering social and emotional support.

Skills acquisition

Agencies have now been set up in most regions in order to develop new Credit Unions and support existing ones.[3] In Britain, regional agencies provide training staff. For example, Santon Credit Union was able to call upon a regional Financial Training Officer, in order to train the new women members acquired as a consequence of the project.

When you're raising a family you become reticent ... you lose confidence and I think everyone of us has discovered that we've got talents that were there all the time but never used (Woman member, quoted in Berthoud and Hinton, 1989).

People have said that they've gone from here to jobs they've applied for on the strength of their Credit Union experience ... we are always giving references out (ibid).

Improved confidence and self-esteem

This was first seen within the official structure of the Credit Union itself. The project built on the core group's existing skills and strengths, and their tremendous networking ability. Their increase in independence and confidence soon showed itself. The project influenced change in the constitution of the Credit Union, challenging male domination at the top; seven months into our project, 66 new members had joined the Credit Union, of which 75 per cent were women. Towards the end of the project, two black women were elected onto the Board of Directors of the Credit Union, which had previously consisted of white men, and one black woman had gained enough confidence to say she was interested in the assistant treasurer's role and began training for this. A white woman took over the role of secretary.

We got voted on the Board of Directors and got invited to a National Conference in Glasgow. We stayed in bed and breakfast and went to a dance. We felt really important. It was great to get away from the kids.

We would never have stood up in front of a crowd and spoken before. Now we do it and it doesn't really bother us that much. It develops your character as well as all the latent gifts that come out of people.

...they sat the three of us at a table on the stage and I was petrified, but I must admit I've never felt so important in all my life [speaking about a local church presentation on credit unions].

The informal results of the group working and socialising appeared immense. One participant reported:

Women in groups can do so much good for each other. Last week one woman cried as she told us her [man] stayed out until 4.00am most nights. Another woman said 'you should be so lucky, mine don't come in till tea-time the next day!' Then it snowballed and in the end, five or six women were talking through the same problem and how they'd tried to tackle it. The first woman ended up laughing.

I can't explain things very well, but before I joined the Credit Union I was miserable as sin because I had a few problems. I used to sit at home all day feeling sorry for myself and fat and ugly. Now I've got something to look forward to ... I'm needed here and I'm [very] good at the work I do. Nobody has ever said that before.

Changes in close relationships

Improved confidence had effects on the women's relationships with male partners or husbands:

The good thing is, I can get a loan for the first time in my life, without asking him first, and I don't have to grovel to a bank manager.

I think coming here [the Credit Union] has done me the world of good. I hadn't been out socially for seven years and I was a lap dog at home ... last Sunday I refused to do the washing up for the first time ever.

He hits me about, and having [Credit Union savings] there gives me a bit of power because I know that I could up and leave him more easily.

Ironically, this increased confidence on the part of women was often perceived as a threat by their menfolk, and additional tensions were experienced in close personal relationships:

He told me 'why do you go up there working for nothing at that bloody Credit Union when you should be here with the kids?'

He told me I was no good at anything, and it was pointless me going for the Board of Directors when I couldn't even add up. I really wanted to prove him wrong, but he didn't praise me up even when I did.

Whilst there is increasing emphasis in literature on the empowerment of women, the pain involved in the process often remains unacknowledged. Women in our group needed support and sometimes physical protection. Feminist social or community work action cannot be based entirely upon increasing personal confidence and power, but must also involve itself in wider campaigns and social action to address the wider context. Some women needed a safe haven due to increased tensions with their partners. Assumptions may be made by community development workers about levels of oppression-awareness; the educative role of workers should not be underestimated.

This finding is confirmed in research which showed that even 'aware men' who had joined men's groups struggled to accept women's empowerment: 'we were in favour of women's independence, but felt threatened by it. We wanted to renounce our aggressive role, but felt bound by it' (Tolson cited in Dominelli and McCleod 1989).

Conclusion

Most literature on Credit Unions, here and in North America, emphasises mainly the economic benefits of Credit Unions. It should be emphasised that the Credit Union movement is neither the only, nor the ultimate, anti-poverty strategy.

What is required as an overall strategy are policies which treat men and women as equal breadwinners, by increasing womens' labour market qualifications and their job chances, by pursuing wage justice for women by increasing income support and services for children ... and by laying to rest forever the dangerous myth that dependency protects women.
(Cass in Glendinning and Millar 1987 p.268)

This paper is a modest feminist addition to the literature, which appeals for the recognition of how women's social well-being and financial and organisational skills are affected by involvement with Credit Unions, whilst acknowledging their acute lack of confidence. I consider the biggest

barrier to such projects to be social scepticism about ordinary people taking on powerful roles. The project emphasised the 'unusual abilities strengths and sustenance of women to develop and administer credit unions throughout the country' (a respondent). Women living in poverty should not be viewed as victims but as 'strong, responsible, self-directed people' (Glendinning and Millar, 1987).

Annette Rimmer works at the Social Work Department, University of Salford, Frederick Road, Salford M6 6PU. Fax: 0161 2952100.

Notes

1 I acknowledge that men also live in poverty, but this study focused on the poverty of women. I also understand that 'women' are not a homogeneous group and are divided by many factors, particularly race.

2 Credit Unions are said to have begun in Germany in 1849, when small farmers found themselves in debt between sowing and reaping. One farmer suggested that they should save together and help each other during hard times. The movement spread quickly, particularly in North America, Ireland, the Caribbean, Africa, and Asia. However, this might be a Eurocentric view of Credit Union history, and most communities throughout the world have developed some form of community saving in times of hardship; just one example is 'pardner schemes' in Caribbean countries.

3 In Britain, these agencies are generally associated to the Association of British Credit Unions, or the National Federation of Credit Unions, which are funded by local government, fund-raising, and contributions from Credit Union bodies in other parts of the world, particularly North America.

References

Albee A (1996) 'Beyond banking for the poor: credit mechanisms and women's empowerment' in *Gender and Development* 4:3, 1996

Birmingham City Council (1990) *Poverty Study.*

Brady (1984) 'Living in debt' in Blamire (ed) *Dealing with Debt.* Birmingham Settlements, 318 Summer Lane (Community organisation).

Channel Four TV, UK (1996) *The Great, the Good and the Dispossessed: a report of the Channel Four Commission on Poverty*, Channel Four, 124 Horseferry Road London SW1 P2TX.

Child Poverty Action Group (1996) *Poverty, Journal of the Child Poverty Action Group* 93.

Doherty P (1981) *Derry Credit Union*, (souvenir booklet).

Donnelly A (1986) *Feminist Social Work with a Women's Group*, University of East Anglia, UK.

Glendinning C and Millar, J (eds) (1987) *Women and Poverty in Britain*, Sussex Wheatsheaf.

Harker and Oppenheim (1996) *Poverty: The Facts*, Child Poverty Action Group.

Kempson (1996) *Life on a Low Income*, Joseph Rowntree Foundation.

McKillop et al (1995) *Local Economy*, 10(1) May 1995.

McRobbie A (1986) 'The Politics of Feminist Research: between talk, text and action', *Feminist Review* 12.

MIND (1992) *Stress on Women.*

Information from Money Advice Centre, Birmingham Settlement, Birmingham.

Pascall (1986) *Social Policy: A Feminist Analysis*, Tavistock.

Pahl(1989) *Money and marriage*, Macmillan.

Tolson cited in Dominelli,L and McCleod, E (1989) *Feminist Social Work*, Macmillan.

Participation begins at home:
adapting participatory development approaches from Southern contexts

Ros David and Yvonne Craig

Participatory appraisal methods have been developed in a Southern context to facilitate the involvement of people in analysing their own situation and seeking solutions to their problems. This article describes a Community Assessment in the UK, in which participatory methods were used effectively to support community residents in putting together a plan for local action.

Many development agencies working in Southern contexts have come to recognise that the essence of good development work is the involvement of people in seeking solutions to their own problems. Time and time again, it has been shown that if people have a stake in, and feel ownership of, an initiative, it is more likely to be both successful and sustainable. Thus, in many contexts in the South, poor people themselves are progressively more involved in analysing their own situation and seeking ways to address their concerns. The process of supporting people as they address issues of social exclusion, low self-esteem, and voicelessness, has become central to NGO work.

In 1995, Oxfam UK/I decided to develop its anti-poverty work in Britain. This decision was prompted by the recognition that some of the root causes of poverty are the same in the North as they are in the South, and the fact that poverty is increasingly understood as more than the absence of material goods and services (Watkins 1996). Another factor influencing

Oxfam UK/I's decision was the recognition that the North could learn from the South. Accordingly, Oxfam UK/I's UK-based programme has supported the exploration of appropriate analytical and conceptual 'tools' which promote the participation of communities. This article will describe an example of using some participatory appraisal tools in Great Hollands housing estate in Bracknell, England, where over 250 people were involved in a Community Assessment exercise. People from the estate met together over the course of a month to carry out an assessment detailing their perceptions, ideas, and concerns about, and aspirations for, the community in which they live. From this, with the support of outside facilitators, they put together an Action Plan to address these issues.

In the article, we examine the process of this Community Assessment. Like any other process, it had its flaws; we explore some of the difficulties we experienced when using participatory methodologies developed in the South, in a Northern context. We also look at the salutary lessons that can be learned from this process for work in both hemispheres, lessons which we hope will contribute to the debates of how best to involve people in a process of participatory development — whether in the North, or South. Finally, we will try to convey the positive experience of initiating a process which seems likely to take on a life, and dynamism, of its own.

Setting the scene

Bracknell is situated approximately 36 miles from London, and lies close to the main motorway route linking London with Wales. Its economy is flourishing as a result of the presence of 'high-tech' computer companies and other light industries. Bracknell was largely built up from the mid-1950s onwards, and was one of the 'new towns' created after the Second World War to provide better living conditions for people from overcrowded slums in Britain's large conurbations. The new towns were intended to be self-contained communities, with housing and industry developed coherently. Bracknell was a town planner's dream (Parris and Parris 1981), made up of a number of housing estates which are each served by a shopping precinct, church, schools, and community centre. Great Hollands was one of the last estates to be built, in 1967. Many of the first residents moved there from the East End of London.

Great Hollands is a thriving housing estate of around 11,000 people. Despite having changed hugely over the years, it has retained its white working-class character. It has a low proportion of ethnic minorities (3 per cent, according to the 1991 census), and a higher than average proportion of unskilled labourers (Babtie Group 1997). Though it had a relatively bad reputation during the 1970s, it has changed over the years, and people are now very happy to live there. The positive aspects of living in Great Hollands shone through during the course of the Community Assessment: it has

Residents of Great Hollands working on the Community Assessment.

Ros David

a low crime rate, good schools, and plenty of green recreational areas.

Despite this, people throughout the estate recognise that there are social problems, which they would like to address. Recent statistics reveal pockets of deprivation. Great Hollands has the highest proportion (over 20 per cent) of primary-school children receiving free school meals in the Borough (Babtie Group 1997). It also has the third highest 'children's support score'[1] in the county, indicating the likelihood of children being taken into state care (Babtie Group 1997).

Methodology

The Great Hollands Community Assessment was mainly facilitated by staff from a small rural development agency, the Community Council of Berkshire (CCB). CCB's mission is to work with the disadvantaged throughout the county. The original initiative for the Community Assessment project came from the local Borough (Municipal) Council, who recognised the need to increase local people's involvement in council policy and develop local Forums. CCB's success, in early 1997, in securing Council funding for a Community Development Worker (CDW), to work alongside local Forums in southern Bracknell, added impetus to the initiative.

The South Bracknell Neighbourhood Community Forum was set up in 1996 by the Borough Council to ensure greater involvement of local residents in local government decisions. The Forum meets quarterly to discuss residents' concerns, and to develop potential solutions. CCB reasoned that the only way to develop the role of community fora was to carry out an assessment to gain understanding of the priorities of local people. With this in mind, the idea of carrying out a Community Assessment, using Participatory Appraisal methods, was put to the Forum by CCB staff and an external consultant during a meeting in June. The Forum members were generally in favour, though initially a little sceptical, of the plan. While many voiced concern about the size and scope of the task, scepticism was tempered by a sense of curiosity.

In response to the issues outlined above, they chose Great Hollands as the estate where the assessment should take place. Seven active Forum members volunteered to help with the assessment;. as one put it, 'we have wanted to have something to get our teeth into for a while, and this assessment could help us take some positive action'. These seven volunteers, plus four CCB staff and one external consultant made up the team which facilitated the Community Assessment.

The assessment was carried out during the month of July 1997. Preparatory work, carried out in June, included meetings with officers and members of the local Borough Council and local residents' groups, and collection and analysis of secondary literature. The assessment began with a public meeting to launch the idea in the community. This meeting marked the beginning of four intensive weeks of interactions between different groups and individuals throughout the Great Hollands estate.

In the course of the assessment, a range of participatory tools were used. These included flow (or contact) diagrams, Venn diagrams, matrices, oral histories, mapping exercises, well-being ranking, and timelines (see Pretty et al, 1995). Efforts were made to involve a cross-section of people: young mothers, single mothers, mothers of children with disabilities, teenage girls, teenage boys, minority groups, working men, unemployed men, single women, and older people. In total over 250 people participated. By the end of the month, at least one person from each street in Great Hollands had been involved. This was felt by the team of facilitators to be an achievement in such a limited period of time.

A final 'feedback' or 'validation' meeting marked the end of the intensive part of the assessment. At this meeting, the Forum

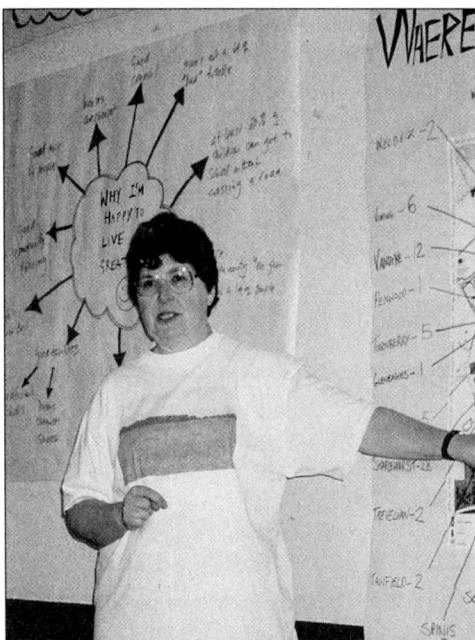

Ros David

Participatory methods facilitate 'real diaglogue' in the community.

members reported back and discussed the problems identified and potential solutions put forward by groups and individuals during the assessment. Concerns and suggestions had been divided by the facilitating team into five groups: those put forward by women and mothers; men and fathers; younger people; older people; and professionals (health workers, social workers, police, teachers, youth workers, etc) working on the estate. Each group had put forward suggestions for a workable plan of action,[2] which was in three sections:

- things that can be done by us and require no help from outside;
- things that we can do with a little help (finance, support etc) from outside;
- projects for which we can seek outside help or funding (for example, local Government grants, or money from the National Lottery).

At this meeting, a core group of 16 people, representing various groups in Great Hollands, volunteered to meet after the summer break to begin planning the next course of action.

The development of participatory approaches in the North and South

Participatory approaches have had a long gestation in international development work. In the 1970s, a body of rapid rural appraisal (RRA) methods began to emerge and coalesce in response to growing dissatisfaction among development workers with traditional quantitative research. During the 1980s, increasing emphasis began to be placed on the importance of empowerment and the sustainability of local action and institutions (Chambers 1997). Subsequently, participatory rural appraisal (PRA) emerged as a distinct methodology.[3] This approach moved away from the concept of 'outsiders' as researchers learning about another culture, and instead emphasised their role as facilitators of a community-led process of listening and interactive learning; the attitude and self-critical awareness of the facilitator is of crucial importance.

The participatory methods used in the South have been developed in the North since the 1980s, when, in Britain as elsewhere, individuals began experimenting with approaches developed internationally. In the North, where the urban context has tended to be of primary importance in research and activism around poverty, the word 'rural' has been dropped, and the term Participatory Appraisal[4] is now generally used to describe this type of approach.

An exciting body of literature — mainly unpublished — documents the recent developments of Participatory Appraisal (PA) approaches in Britain. PA has been used widely, particularly in the health arena, to create a better match between health needs and health provision (see

Cornwall 1997, Sellers and Westerby 1996, Cresswell 1996). Projects associated with mental health, HIV and AIDS are also experimenting with participatory methods (Weaver 1996). Small groups in Scotland have been experimenting with the use of PA methods in a variety of settings, including the development of fishery management strategies, the analysis of the use of space with groups of young people, the development of local Agenda 21 projects, work with housing associations, and the development of forestry policy (Weaver 1996, Jones 1996, Jones: personal communication). Unfortunately, despite these initiatives, there is still a dearth of analytical information available about PA experiences in the North (Craig and Barahona 1996).

Reactions to participatory tools in Great Hollands

Despite some difficulties, which we discuss below, the Community Assessment in Great Hollands was a resounding success. Most people — particularly the shyer and less articulate — tended to enjoy both group and individual participatory sessions. During the course of the assessment, many people commented on the amount of information that had been generated, the intricacy of the diagrams or matrices, and the way the methods encouraged greater involvement. 'This was much more interesting than I thought it would be', confided one elderly woman; 'usually community meetings are about us all sitting and listening to local politicians.'

The Neighbourhood Forum members were so pleased with the process that they are currently asking CCB for support in carrying out assessments on other estates in the area. Forum members have requested further training in participatory approaches, and appreciate the way that these methods facilitate 'real dialogue', as one put it, in the community.

Despite some initial scepticism, most people who took part in the assessment were delighted with the final, documented results. Formalising the diagrams from what could only be described as 'scruffy flip-chart paper' to A4 overhead transparencies gave the assessment an air of professionalism which was clearly welcome. Many people commented on how much they enjoyed seeing their ideas legitimised in type. 'Now we can show our ideas to the local authority', said one woman.

However, the reactions were not always positive. The absence of questionnaires and armies of surveyors was disappointing for some. People in Great Hollands are generally literate, and participatory tools have largely been developed for work in non-literate communities. In general, middle-aged men, particularly professional men (both residents of Great Hollands and those working on the estate) were most likely to be sceptical of the approach. As one person commented: 'this is social workers' clap trap [nonsense].'

However, questioning the authenticity of the approach was a healthy reaction. In a Northern context it is much more likely that sentiments of this kind will be expressed. The unequal power relations, which often accompany PRAs in the South, (where external agencies are associated with highly prized outside funding), often influence people's compliance. In contrast, our presence as facilitators in Great Hollands was not accompanied by any promise of outside funding or substantial support. Such questioning is an indication of the more even balance of power between facilitators and community groups. It could be seen as a necessary prerequisite to a deeper ownership of the process.

Unfortunately, time constraints prevented us from exploring other methods and approaches, which might have been more acceptable to certain elements in the community. Initial ideas had included the use of video cameras, but lack of time prevented this. One digression from traditional participatory approaches was made when a male member of the facilitating team wanted to carry out a formal questionnaire in his immediate neighbourhood. Another brief foray was made into using photo collage: teenage girls were given a camera to document their perception of Great Hollands, or, as they put it, 'chilling out [relaxing] on the estate'. This proved highly successful.

A gender-balanced approach?

The difficulty of involving women in participatory approaches is well-documented in the development literature: 'the participation of women has in all PRAs been limited and discontinuous' (Mosse 1995, 573, in the context of Western India). In the context of Scotland, '...in almost every context it proved harder, in a short time, to locate and find the time to talk to women, especially younger women' (Wallace 1994, 12). Interestingly, this was not our experience in Great Hollands. Women seemed more interested than men were in finding out how they could get involved in community action, and played a dominant role in both facilitating the work of the Community Assessment (outnumbering men by eight to three in the facilitating team), and participating in meetings and discussions.

Many men work away from the estate for long hours, and this was one reason why it was much easier to involve women in the process as they were more likely to be present on the estate during the day. Arrangements were made to meet up with groups and individuals at times that were mutually convenient. Meetings with women tended to take place during the day (at school groups, play groups, at their homes in the late afternoon or during a break in their working day). Meetings with men (particularly working men) were often in the evenings and in public areas. Where possible, facilitators also tried to involve residents in informal, ad-hoc ways (in the shopping centre, after church, etc).

The chief concerns of women and mothers (in random order) were as follows:

debt; isolation (from the community, if you work, and from other people if you don't work); lack of extended family; pockets of deprivation; lack of affordable childcare; lack of local, cheap activities for children of all ages; lack of provision for children with special needs; lack of special activity for women; glass on the children's playground; difficulty of getting out of Great Hollands; dog faeces on the pavements; headlice infestation at school; unsafe underpasses; poor provision of non-fiction titles, to help with children's schoolwork, in the library; the need for tarmacing and effective drainage in the car park.

The chief concerns of men and father (again, in random order) were: personal safety of families; vandalism; insufficient car-parking spaces, and the failure to delineate parking bays in the squares; the need for tarmacing and good lighting in the car park; dog faeces on grass verges and recreation areas; difficulty of car access to the recreation ground; failure to prune bushes and trees, especially around lights, and bad lighting in general, particularly in the underpasses, which adds to safety problems; cycle-paths not directed into town centre; lack of litter bins; 'rat-runs' [short cuts taken by motorists] through the estate making roads unsafe.

Without wanting to either over-generalise or over-emphasise consensual views, a broad distinction can be made between the concerns put forward by women and mothers in the community, and those put forward by men and fathers. Women were generally more concerned with social elements of community life, such as debt, isolation, and pockets of deprivation. Women and mothers were also typically more worried about facilities for their children: both for young children and for the teenagers who 'lark about the estate at night'. In contrast, professional men and fathers were mainly concerned with practical issues, such as car-parking, cycle paths, street lighting, and vandalism. This may be because men found it easier to talk about practical concerns to which practical solutions could be applied. It may also be because women more readily interpreted 'community' as meaning the social nexus, rather than the physical environment. Women undoubtedly shared men's concerns about practical issues, such as street lighting, but these were not the first issues that they chose to discuss. It is interesting that no clear distinction can be made between the concerns of older men and older women: both were principally preoccupied with 'the loutish behaviour of youths today', personal isolation, and fear of crime.

Listening to women in male-dominated hierarchies

Although women were heavily involved in the analysis and in putting together the action plan, it remains to be seen whether women's voices will be heard in the final analysis. As is so often the case in local politics, Bracknell Forest Borough Council and Bracknell Town Council are dominated by men. At some stage, action points from each of the five groups will need to be prioritised and decisions made about taking issues forward. CCB's previous experience has shown that women often participate in an assessment and initiate action. However, ultimately it is councillors — mostly male — who are in control of financial resources.

Learning lessons from the work in Bracknell

This brief experience of using participatory methods in Great Hollands threw up a number of interesting insights, which are, undoubtedly, as relevant to working in the South as they are to working in the North. While lack of space prevents a fuller discussion, four learning points stand out:

Time is of the essence

The much-quoted remark 'just ask, they know; and they are your friends' (Pottier 1991, quoted in Mosse, 1995) reveals much that is unfortunate about many participatory processes. The rapidity with which many participatory appraisals are carried out undermines the ability of outside facilitators to listen (particularly to contradictions and the unexpected), to be flexible in response to local ideas and, crucially, to allow (and indeed encourage) people to become gradually more involved in the process. Lack of time can result in a failure to reveal unequal power relations, and different perceptions of reality.

Time was an issue in Great Hollands. Despite working in our own culture, in our own language, and having a thorough understanding of local political structures, it took a surprising amount of time to understand local dynamics, hierarchies, and history. We had not come to Great Hollands with money to offer; just the offer of support to Forum members in carrying out the assessment. We needed to build trust quickly, to empathise, to create a bond, and adapt our manner and behaviour according to whomever we happened to be speaking. Indeed, we could not have successfully facilitated the assessment if there had not been a CDW, based in Great Hollands for a year, to support the process.

Time was a problem for everyone. Even those community members who were keen to be involved in the assessment found the commitment difficult to sustain. The Forum team members involved throughout the process had to juggle their schedules continually. Everyone had their own lives to lead, with the usual round of parental duties, work commitments, and social engagements. They could not be expected to clear their diaries. While this is all too easy to forget in other people's contexts and cultures, in our own, it is much more difficult. Each interview or meeting took at least two hours. In the evening, after a working day, two hours is a long time to give up to a process with an uncertain outcome.

Each context is set in its own political web

Another issue, which is all too often downplayed or ignored by researchers working in other cultures, was the complexity of local politics. Political intrigue was rife in Great Hollands during the period of the assessment, as recent local elections had resulted in the party previously in control of local government being replaced. Inevitably, policy was rapidly changing as the incoming council began to create its own strategy. These political upheavals inevitably affected the assessment, since the support of the local council for the outcome would be crucial to its success. It was vital that the process did not become hi-jacked by those with political interests. The assessment was also vulnerable to the legacy of past political campaigning; each issue (be it roads, lighting or local housing developments) had its own party-political 'label', since one or other councillor had covered it in his or her manifesto.

Steering the assessment through the political minefield became an aim in itself. Two factors helped in this: first, the avoidance of too many public fora which could be dominated by political figures, and secondly the fact that the Forum members involved in the assessment took an active role in deftly steering the process away from party politics, regardless of their many personal political differences. Without this help, the assessment could have easily been derailed.

The myth of community consensus

Just as the whole nature of 'community' has been challenged in the development literature, so too should it be scrutinised here. It became clear, over time, that the Great Hollands estate is divided both geographically and socially. Those who live in Great Hollands south often protest at their address being given as 'Great Hollands', preferring to call their area by its street name of Staplehurst. Well-being ranking carried out during the assessment illustrated a huge

social and economic gulf between different sectors of the estate. A 'high well-being' ranking for some implies a good (professional) job, owner-occupied house, and plenty of surplus income. For others, this ranking signified at least one adult in employment (probably as an unskilled worker), a council flat, and eligibility for state benefits.

A second point on consensus is that, while participatory approaches encourage the exploration of social diversity and conflicting perspectives, the analysis all too often masks heterogeneity. A huge amount of information, and a variety of perspectives, were aired and discussed during the course of the assessment. However, in the final analysis, this information was distilled into five perspectives (mothers/women; men/fathers; older people; younger people; and professionals). The aim of the assessment was to produce an action plan, and this was achieved. Producing a summary is inherent in every planning process; it is a prerequisite to practical application. However, there will always remain a tension between retaining a sense of community diversity, and producing summary reports for action.

Adaptation is necessary in a Northern context

Individuals and institutions throughout Britain are currently developing a plethora of participatory approaches. The essence of good PA — listening, self-critical awareness, encouraging people to take control — will never be inappropriate. Many of the reasons why participatory tools are popular in the South are equally relevant in the North. Participatory methods emphasise listening to people, and giving them the opportunity to analyse their own situation and seek their own course of action. Feeling enthusiastic and positive about taking action inspires people with energy. (The downside of this, of course, is that people can feel cheated when change turns out to be more difficult to bring about than initially anticipated.)

Although PA methods are potentially both valuable and appropriate in a Northern context, they could further benefit from adaptation to a new setting, and to meet the demands (and expectations) in a postmodern age. Other methods could be used to complement traditional PRA tools. It would be interesting to experiment with methods that entail limited time commitment, and give opportunities for creativity, such as video and audio tape, drama, and art.

Concluding remarks

As always, with the benefit of hindsight, the process of this specific assessment could have been improved. More time, more training (of the Forum members), greater involvement of more residents – the list could continue. However, despite its flaws, the assessment has already yielded some interesting results.

Residents from Great Hollands have recently held a well-attended open meeting, at which they sub-divided into teams to take forward five tasks. Residents are also applying for a local council award, to cover the initial costs of putting together a local newsletter. The Neighbourhood Forum has requested further training from the CCB so that they can carry out assessments in other neighbourhoods. One of the major issues, which seemed to concern everybody, was the state of the community centre. Recent activity, by a group of residents, has resulted in a pledge of money and, more importantly, a seat at the table with Borough officers planning the redevelopment of the centre.

Fortunately, the CCB Community Development Worker is based in Great Hollands to support and encourage the continuing process; in the North just as in the South, follow-up and support is essential for lasting success.

Ros David is an independent consultant. She formerly worked for Oxfam and has widespread experience of using participatory methodologies

in the South. Contact details: 37 Hayfield Road, Oxford OX2 6TX. Tel/fax +44 (0)1865 559798. E-mail: davidccoates@gn.apc.org

Yvonne Craig works as a Community Development Worker for the Community Council of Berkshire (CCB). For the last two years, she has been adapting and using participatory methodologies in the Northern context. Contact details: Community Council of Berkshire. Epping House, 55 Russell Street, Reading RG1 7XG. Tel: +44 (0)118 9612000;fax: +44 (0)118 9612600

Notes

1 The 'children's support score' was developed by Bebbington and Miles to forecast the likelihood of children being admitted into the care of the local authorities. The score is based on a number of factors (1991 Census data about single parent families, 4+ children, ethnic group, tenure, overcrowding, age of children, receipt of benefits) about the children's background which are weighted according their importance.

2 Because of lack of space, the concerns and potential solutions put forward by each of these groups are not given in detail. They are available in summary form from the CCB.

3 The evolution and spread of both RRA and PRA methods are well documented (IIED, 1988-to present).

4 During the 1980s, a distinction between methods emerged in the North similar to the RRA-PRA split in Southern contexts. While Participatory Assessment (PA) gave more emphasis to community-based learning and action, Rapid Participatory Appraisal (RPA) became more systematised. RPA is characterised as 'a professional-led rapid research approach that aims to furnish health managers with an understanding of communities' (Cornwall 1997, 3).

References

Babtie group (1997) 'Bracknell Forest needs profile: Initial results for discussion', Report for the Babtie group, Bracknell, Berkshire, July

Chambers, Robert (1997) *Whose Reality Counts: Putting the Last First*, ITDG Publications, London

Cornwall, A (1997) 'Roundshaw participation well being needs assessment', Report for Merton, Sutton and Wandsworth Special Health Promotion Services, April

Craig, Y and C Barahona (1996) *Perceptions of East Berkshire: A Rapid Assessment*, CCB Research and Policy Paper, No 1, Community Council of Berkshire, Reading

Cresswell, T (1996) 'Participatory appraisal in the UK urban health sector: keeping faith with perceived needs', *Development in Practice* 6:1, February

IIED (1988) *RRA Notes*, International Institute of Environment and Development, London (*RRA Notes* became *PLA Notes* in 1995)

Jones, C (1996) 'Wallyford, participatory forestry appraisal', unpublished report to Reafforesting Scotland, Rural Forum and Highlands and Islands Forum to the Scottish office.

Mosse, D (1995) 'Authority, gender and knowledge: theoretical reflections on participatory rural appraisal', *Economic and Political Weekly*, 18 March

Parris H and J Parris (1981) *The Idea of New Towns*, Bracknell Development Corporation, Bracknell, England

Pretty, J, Guijt, I, Thompson, J and Scoones, I (1995) *Participatory Learning and Action: A Trainer's Guide*, IIED, London

Sellers, T and M Westerby (1996) 'Teenage facilitators: barriers to improving adolescent sexual health', *PLA Notes*, IIED, London, February

Wallace, T (1994) 'PRA: Some issues raised by experience in the North', Paper for DSA conference, Lancaster, Sept.

Watkins, K (1995) *The Oxfam Poverty Report*, Oxfam, Oxford

Weaver, J (1996) 'The use of participatory rural appraisal in the UK: A brief overview', report for the Charities Evaluation Service, December

The street press:
homelessness, self-help, and social identity

Tessa Swithinbank

During the 1990s, the street press movement has spread rapidly throughout the developed world. The movement is a unique social experiment which tackles the problems of homelessness through the concept of self-help. Helping homeless, ex-homeless and vulnerably accommodated people help themselves through the selling of newspapers or magazines can break dependency on state benefits, and is an alternative to begging.

When the feasibility of *The Big Issue* initiative was first discussed between its instigators in the private sector,[1] and a wide range of concerned people (including homeless people themselves, workers in non-governmental organisations working on homelessness, representatives of local government, and the police), many said that the idea was unworkable. The concept aroused intense suspicion, even among homeless people themselves. The perspective of many professionals already working on the issue of homelessness was also negative. Their reasoning was two-fold: first, that there were already enough charities and projects caring for the immediate and long-term needs of homeless people in the UK; and second, that such a 'commercial' idea would never catch on. *The Big Issue* initiative takes an empowerment perspective, focusing on homeless people not simply as social problems, but as contributors to their own future.

This article surveys the development of the initiative, and compares *The Big Issue* to street papers in North, South and Eastern Europe, and South Africa. It also discusses why gender, race, and other aspects of social identity affect the likelihood of homeless people choosing to sell street publications as a strategy for survival or for leaving the streets.

The Big Issue initiative

The Big Issue was launched in September 1991, with capital from The Body Shop Foundation, the charitable arm of a well-known UK-based toiletries and cosmetics company, which itself has a socially responsible business policy.[2] It began with 25 vendors, and a monthly print-run of 30,000 copies, published in English. At first, the newspaper was sold only in London.

Word soon spread on the streets, and within a few months hundreds of homeless people were selling *The Big Issue*. On its first anniversary the change was made to a fortnightly publication, and from a newspaper to a magazine format, in response to both consumer and vendor preference for this smaller size. Since 1993, it has been published weekly. Three further regional publications — *Big Issue Scotland*, *Big Issue Cymru* (Wales) and *Big Issue in the North* — have since been launched.

Sustainability and enterprise

An important element in the sustainability of *The Big Issue* is its high quality, which means that consumers want to buy and read it on a regular basis. *The Big Issue* has achieved this through a lively combination of investigative reporting, campaigning on issues that affect homeless people, arts news, and celebrity interviews with such people as the British Prime Minister, Tony Blair, and the pop star George Michael.

The London edition has an ABC (Audited Bureau of Circulation) sales figure of 149,194 per week, with the national figure standing at over 300,000. Independent readership surveys reveal that the average buyer is middle-income and under 40, and about 55 per cent of readers are women. *The Big Issue* is read every week nationally by over a million people. Sales provide 60 per cent of the magazine's income, and advertising provides the other 40 per cent.

A holistic approach to homelessness

Homelessness is not an isolated social issue. It is a direct consequence of social and economic pressures on individuals. The recession, unemployment, lack of affordable accommodation, mortgage default, marital breakdown, and abuse at home are contributory factors to a person's becoming homeless. Although Britain is a 'welfare state', the state benefit system has been drastically cut back over the last decade, making it impossible to do more than subsist on government benefit. People who sleep on the streets only receive a personal weekly allowance of about £25 (*Big Issue* unpublished information). *The Big Issue* initiative responds in a holistic way to homelessness.

Income generation through sales

Vendors buy the magazine for 35p (the price of a pint of milk) and sell it for 80p. They are given a badge, sales training, allocated a 'pitch' from which to sell, and they sign a code of conduct. Around 500 vendors sell in London on any one day, with a further 3,000 in all major UK towns and cities. For some vendors, selling *The Big Issue* is a central element of their strategy for making a living; for others, it plays a more minor role.

The social initiative

The social initiative activities provide a support system to suit the needs of each vendor, and create the opportunity for re-integration into society. All vendors have access to a range of support services, run by a number of teams which differ in detail in each region. In London, Vendor Services offers housing and resettlement, from emergency accommodation to permanent housing with resettlement support; a Drug and Alcohol Worker offers counselling to vendors who are worried about their drug or alcohol use, and provides a referral service to specialist agencies; and a Vendor Liaison Worker handles day-to-day issues and suggests services which may be of use.

Outreach teams offer practical and emotional support to homeless people, both on the streets and at *The Big Issue* offices. A Vendor Support Fund gives small grants to vendors who may need, for example, furniture for a new flat, special clothing for a new job, or equipment for training. The Jobs Education and Training Unit can help vendors move into the workplace or further education. The unit not only provides individual programmes for vendors who want to learn keyboard and computing skills, word processing or desk top publishing, but also finds and funds places on training and education courses and offers work experience opportunities, in *The Big Issue* offices and in other companies.

Self-expression and awareness-raising

A range of creative workshops help homeless people rebuild their self-confidence; these include writing and drama groups, and art, photography, and video workshops. *The Big Issue* is a forum where homeless people can air their views and publish their work. The flourishing creative writing group has been meeting weekly since the magazine's launch, providing copy for the two-page 'Street Lights' section in the magazine.

Impact of *The Big Issue*

At international level, *The Big Issue* was nominated as one of the 100 Urban Best Practices at the UN Habitat II Conference in May 1996, reflecting its impact both nationally and internationally on effecting social change. Yet the precise impact of the magazine on the lives of the homeless is difficult to estimate. The initiative works with only a minority of the thousands of UK homeless; selling *The Big Issue* is not a possibility for every homeless person: vendors need to be physically and mentally active to be able to stand on the streets all day.

We have not, so far, kept detailed statistics of the numbers of men and women who sell the magazine and take part in related social activities. Vendors often move on into jobs or training without informing us, or simply cease selling. There are vendors who have been selling since *The Big Issue* was launched, but others who do so for only a few months or weeks. Others may sell for a while, stop, and then start selling again.

The Big Issue's own definition of success is to provide an opportunity for people to help themselves. Vendors have a variety of expectations; while for some homeless people success is securing formal employment, and involvement in *The Big Issue* is one step towards this, for others simply selling the paper is a big personal achievement. In terms of earning money, *The Big Issue* has given homeless people a legal way of making money, as an alternative to criminal activities such as begging or theft. The police in various parts of the country have commented that petty crime has been reduced in inner cities because of *The Big Issue* (*Big Issue* internal information).

Aside from the economic benefits of the sales themselves, many sellers stated (in the Vendors' Survey) that one of the most rewarding aspects of selling the magazine is their day-to-day contact with the general public. This has been a very positive way of counteracting the sense of invisibility that homeless people experience. Vendors reported that selling has also increased their self-respect and confidence.

In terms of public education, *The Big Issue* has contributed greatly to placing homelessness in the forefront of national consciousness. The magazine promotes change in the relationship between the public and homeless people, through challenging stereotypical attitudes. These attitudes have a strong element of ambiguity: many people, for example, feel sorry for people on the streets, but dislike being approached by them for money, and may perceive them as dirty or lazy (*Big Issue* internal information).

Homelessness and social identity

Homelessness in the UK is essentially a male phenomenon; while national statistics on homeless applications are not broken down by gender, evidence can be culled from various research reports (Aldridge 1996). Although homelessness among women is growing, they tend to find ways of staying off the streets. Women make up the majority of 'hidden homeless': sleeping on friends' floors, or trapped in insecure and overcrowded accommodation, in a double bind of poverty and violent personal relationships.

According to a report by the Sainsbury Centre for Mental Health (December 1996) the main differences between homeless men and homeless women are:

- The average age of homeless women is lower than men — a much higher proportion are under 25.
- Women are more likely to have been married, to have had children, and to have maintained contact with their families.
- Women are more likely to have a history of family violence, or abusive relationships with partners (a 1993 report indicated that up to four in ten homeless women had been sexually abused).

- Women are more likely to have been separated from their parents before the age of 10.
- Women are more likely to have stayed on at school, and to have obtained qualifications and work experience.
- Women are more likely to have been diagnosed as schizophrenic.
- Women are much less likely to have problems with alcohol.

Many of these points were confirmed by the results of a survey of 100 *Big Issue* vendors (Dane 1997).

Making the street press friendlier to women

Is the street press an appropriate strategy to address the needs of homeless women? In terms of gender breakdown, 88 per cent of active vendors in London are male and 12 per cent are female. The average age is 34, with two-thirds between 26 and 45 (Vendors' Survey).

It would be difficult to ascertain why women who have once sold *The Big Issue* stop selling, as they are not then available for interview. However, the particular issues affecting women on the streets indicate the reasons for women's low level of participation. First, the experience of women in the informal sector all over the world is that street-selling is difficult for those with small children to care for (Heyzer 1981). In addition, in the UK it is illegal to sell on the streets when accompanied by children aged between five and sixteen (the ages between which schooling is compulsory). Few crèches are available.

Second, homeless women face specific difficulties in relation to violence; many have experienced domestic violence in the past, followed by harassment and sexual threats once they move outside the home, both on the streets or in hostels. Women who have already experienced domestic violence do not feel secure about selling on the streets, where some have been propositioned or attacked.

The Big Issue initiative is responding to this by attempting to create a more women-friendly environment at *The Big Issue* offices, with a 'women's drop-in', where women can come during the afternoon to relax and talk. Women's hostels are also being targeted, to encourage more women to sell, and research is being carried out on how street selling can be made a safe activity for women. More widely, *The Big Issue* initiative is also trying to raise awareness of women's homelessness in order to counter the very male image of homelessness.

Promoting re-integration into society

One of the central issues is how to get homeless people to 'move on', back into mainstream society, and not become dependent on *The Big Issue*. While selling could potentially provide a sustainable income, it should be regarded more as a 'bridge into the world of work'. By selling and taking advantage of the support services, vendors can achieve a degree of stability and begin to make plans for the future. People are encouraged to move on, but this may take one person a month, and another five years.

Having established good working relationships with other agencies, *The Big Issue* initiative is now involved in campaigns, in particular through the Homeless Network (incorporating other UK NGOs working on homelessness, including Shelter and Centrepoint). Street papers themselves take part in campaigning, on issues such as votes for homeless people (in the UK, voters must appear on an electoral register, with a street address).

The street press in other countries

Street papers are a phenomenon of the developed world, where the main street activity for marginalised people is begging. North

Street papers from (left to right) Australia, South Africa, the UK, and Russia.

America and Europe support the greatest number of street papers — nearly 120. Indeed, one of the most distinctive features of the European street paper movement is the fact that most countries support more than one paper: Germany has over 30, and even the Netherlands, with a population of just 15 million, has seven. Diversity is the hallmark of Europe's street papers, with differences in editorial content, circulation figures, size, and status. Some are supported by charities, others are extensions of existing homeless projects, and a few operate as non-profit businesses.

Whilst Britain, Germany and France have the highest numbers of homeless people, statistics indicate that in Southern Europe the family still plays an important social role, and therefore indigenous homelessness, whilst growing, is not as acute (UN 1995). Many homeless people in Southern Europe are refugees and consequently it is this group, along with other marginalised groups, which mainly sells street papers. Refugees have become very visible on the streets of Italian and Greek cities in the past few years, arriving from Albania, Africa, and the former Yugoslavia.

Das Megaphon, the street paper in Graz, Austria, for example, is sold mainly by Nigerian men, not Austrians, and *Terre di Mezzo* in Milan, Italy, is sold mostly by Senegalese men, rather than Italians. In Lisbon, *CAIS* is distributed to different organisations working with marginalised people, whether homeless, ex-drug addicts, ex-prisoners, slum residents, long-term unemployed or the disabled. Support services are therefore tailored towards the needs of these particular groups.

The informal street economic sector in the South does not preclude the sale of street papers, but these are an addition to the existing micro-economies, which are not an option for most homeless people living in the North due to legal regulations prohibiting these activities. (In the UK, there is a law dating from the eighteenth century which allows printed material and periodicals to be sold on the streets.)

In 1996, *Concern* was launched in the Gambia, sold by young men on the beaches. *Big Issue Australia* was launched in Melbourne in June 1996, and is now being sold in Sydney.

Big Issue Cape Town became the second South African street paper in December 1996, the first being *Homeless Talk*, based in Johannesburg. In South Africa, a homeless adult is defined as 'a person of the streets'; while extreme poverty is experienced by many dwellers in former black townships, the poverty and alienation of South Africans on the streets is acute. One of the critical features is that these people are likely to have lost all or most connections to their family. They are likely to suffer from very poor or no self-esteem. In the view of the social development co-ordinator, Debi Diamond, this reflects the legacy of decades of oppressive apartheid and the erosion of self-confidence. The main challenges for the Cape Town paper have been to motivate the vendors to progress beyond the point of generating only enough income for subsistence, and to build their self-esteem.

During the month of April 1997, out of a total of 184 registered vendors, only nine were female, but in fact only four of these were active. In terms of ethnicity, 34 per cent are Xhosa, 33 per cent 'coloured' (the South African term for mixed race) and Afrikaans-speaking, and 33 per cent white, speaking either English or Afrikaans. These statistics reflect the developing impoverishment of white South Africans.

Big Issue Cape Town seeks to challenge and change public perceptions of the role of homeless people in society. Public antagonism still exists towards the homeless, and vendors have suffered from abuse. This is compounded by racial overtones between the different ethnic groups. *Big Issue Cape Town* is addressing these issues but as a new business, it will take time to produce concrete results.

Central and Eastern Europe

The street paper concept is still in its infancy in Central and Eastern Europe. The collapse of communism brought to light previously hidden homelessness in the region. The communist authorities considered homeless people criminals — and this attitude was shared by the general public. However, things are slowly changing. The causes of homelessness throughout Eastern Europe are myriad: ex-prisoners and ex-army people with no family to return to; abuse at home; changing family forms and enforced separation within extended families, unaffordable accommodation, and the low quality of housing stock. A recent report exposes the massive scale of the housing crisis in the countries of Central and Eastern Europe: 'compared with the situation in the EU, the most striking feature of housing exclusion ... is that it is far more

difficult for homeless people to find a way out of their predicament, because the opportunities for access to appropriate assistance are so limited' (Avramov 1997). *Flaszter* was launched in Budapest, Hungary, in January 1997, where at least 20,000 people are homeless, and *Ulica* was recently launched in Warsaw, Poland.

St Petersburg, Russia, has probably the most acute homelessness problem in Eastern Europe, with at least 50,000 people homeless (Nochlyezhka, undated). Alcohol poisoning and malnutrition, combined with the long and brutal winters, are the cause of over 3,000 deaths on the streets each year. The city's street paper, *The Depths*, was launched in 1994, inspired by a copy of *The Big Issue* which arrived via Germany at the night shelter and soup kitchen, (Nochlyezhka). Valeriy Sokolov, founder of the shelter and of *The Depths*, has campaigned and won many rights for homeless people, from the local government.

Since there is no welfare system in St Petersburg for those without an 'internal passport' (which the homeless do not have), those homeless people who come to the shelters are absolutely destitute. The shelter provides food and then gives people the opportunity to earn an income through selling the paper. This has had repercussions for the paper's economic stability, as many vendors are unable to buy their copies initially and the organisation has had to subsidise the paper. There are few women vendors. Freezing winter temperatures also mean that no vendor can stand out on the street, so this presents additional problems of obtaining an income in the winter months. They can stand in the metros, just inside stations.

The Big Issue Scotland recently formed a partnership with *The Depths* with the help of ODA (now the Department for International Development) funding. This is an example of helping to develop projects in Eastern Europe by providing technical and financial help from the West.

Street papers: the future

Street papers would not be an appropriate strategy for tackling homelessness in every country. Where the market of the streets is competitive, or where there is not a high literacy rate among consumers, they would not provide a viable source of income for vendors. They need initial investment, a strong team composed of professional journalists and those working in the social arena, and they need to be economically sustainable, or they will not survive. In addition, the strategy will be more viable for some homeless people than others, depending on factors of social identity including gender and race. Another determinant of whether a street paper will succeed is the public attitude to street selling.

While street papers are not going to eradicate homelessness, they enable individuals to regain a stake in society, and play a large part in raising the profile of homelessness among the public and government officials. As John Bird, founder of *The Big Issue*, observed, the success of street papers is unfortunately built on the tragedy of homelessness. But the initiative represents hope and resolve, in place of defeat and despair.

Tessa Swithinbank is Co-ordinator of International Network of Street Papers and Manager of the International Department, The Big Issue, Fleet House, 57 Clerkenwell Road, London EC1M 5NP. Fax: 00 44 171 418 0428, e-mail: london@bigissue.co.uk

References

Aldridge R (1996) *European Observatory: National Report 1996 for the UK on Youth Homelessness*, FEANTSA,

Avramov D (1997) *Housing Exclusion in Central and Eastern Europe*, Federation of National Organisations Working with the Homeless (FEANTSA), 1 Rue Defacqz, Brussels B-1050, Belgium. Tel: 322-538-6669. Fax: 322-539-4174. e-mail: 106043.1514@compuserve.com,

Dane K (1997) *The Big Issue Vendor Survey*.

Heyzer C (1981) *Women, Subsistence and the Informal Sector. Towards a Framework of Analysis*, IDS Discussion Paper 193, University of Sussex.

Nochlezhka (publisher) *Petersburg in the Early 90s: Crazy, Cold, Cruel* PO Box 110, 191025, St Petersburg, Russia.

Sainsbury Centre for Mental Health (1996) *Double Exposure: Addressing the Needs of Homeless Women with Mental Illness.* December 1996

Useful addresses

The International Network of Street Papers (INSP) was founded in July 1994. Membership is based on being a signatory of the Street Paper Charter. For information contact: INSP c/o The Big Issue, 57 Clerkenwell Road, London EC1M 5NP.
Tel: 171-418-0418. Fax: 171-418-0428.

INSP e-mail: insp.lon@bigissue.co.uk

North American Street Newspapers Association Website:
http://www.speakeasy.org/nasna

National Coalition for the Homeless, 1612 K St NW, No 1004, Washington DC 20006, USA. Tel: 202-775 1322. Fax: 202-775 1316. http://nch.ari.net.

Notes

1 The chairman of the UK company The Body Shop, Gordon Roddick, bought a copy of New York's street paper, *Street News* (launched in 1989), on a trip to the US, and believed that this concept could be developed in the UK.

2 'Socially responsible' is defined here as running a business ethically: a critical part of this is avoiding the exploitation of people involved in the business as suppliers, staff or consumers, or polluting or endangering the environment.

Giving women the credit:
the Norwich Full Circle Project

Ruth Pearson and Erika Watson

The Full Circle Project is a response by a women's organisation to the dynamics of women's poverty and economic exclusion in contemporary Britain. The authors emphasise the need for credit provision for women to be seen as only one part of an integrated strategy for poverty reduction.

Development analysts and practitioners are familiar with the exponential growth of microcredit and other microfinance strategies targeted at poor households in both urban and rural communities in the South over the last decade. Because of the ways in which household gender relations are structured, and especially because of women's role as guarantor of household subsistence needs, many of these programme are particularly focused on women, who have proved to be active participants in such schemes, and particularly good loan repayers (Goetz and Sen Gupta 1996). Since the Microcredit Summit in February 1997, there has been growing international clamour to promote credit for small businesses as a strategy to eradicate poverty and to 'empower' women, in South and North. The Grameen Bank in Bangladesh, which operates on the basis of group collateral and peer pressure, has often been presented as a model to be replicated in other contexts.

Credit is not a magic missing link between poverty and economic sustainability (Johnson and Rogaly 1997). However, as the Full Circle Project suggests, it can be one part of an integrated strategy aimed at providing options for low-income women in the North to break through the structures of economic and social exclusion which are characteristic of late twentieth-century Britain.

Women and poverty in Britain; where micro-credit fits in

In the North, as in Southern economies, the characteristics of women and low-income households are extremely varied, and no single policy approach is appropriate for all. There are many factors which have contributed to the feminisation of poverty in the UK over the last 20 years. The erosion of the level of real wages,[1] particularly at the less skilled end of the labour market where women with children typically cluster, has meant that it is difficult for women to re-enter paid employment after a break for child care, at a level at which a single wage will move her beyond benefit dependency

(MacFarlane 1997); hence the current pre-occupation with welfare-to-work[2] paths for single parents. Although women earn 80 per cent of the average male wage, if they get a job it is more likely to be part-time; a feature of the increasing 'flexibility' of the contemporary labour market (Balls 1993).

Twenty years ago, a low-income household was likely either to have a single wage coming in, or to have one family member who was looking for work, since the value of a single wage could lift a household above poverty level (Gregg and Wadsworth, 1995). Low-income households were thus either still connected, or potentially able to re-connect on receipt of a single wage, with the world of work and other social and economic networks. Today, in contrast, single- or dual-parent households living on the margins of the mainstream economy are more likely to be struggling to survive outside formal employment. This means not only low income, but concentration in localities and regions of high levels of social and economic deprivation: poor housing, badly resourced schools, scarcity of affordable transport and community services, and very limited financial, educational, and training opportunities.

There are other reasons why women find themselves marginalised. Not only single parenthood, but marriage and divorce can also result in women becoming detached from educational, employment, and other services and networks, often despite a previous successful employment or educational history. Migrant women, and those from linguistic and ethnic minorities, face discrimination in access to training and financial services as well as in employment markets, which frequently fail to value their experience and qualifications gained elsewhere (Macfarlane 1997). It is not surprising, therefore, that not only are women amongst the most disadvantaged in poor communities, but that women who are excluded from mainstream markets are concentrated in poor communities.

What then are the options for women trying to re-connect with the mainstream economy? The Full Circle Project is an initiative which has been developed in response to this need by the Women's Employment, Enterprise and Training Unit (WEETU), a women's organisation set up in 1987 to respond to the increasing marginalisation of women in the local economy in the city of Norwich and the surrounding area in eastern England. WEETU's aim was to help women to adapt to economic change by lobbying local and national government, by participating in economic planning at the local level, and by working with statutory training providers to ensure women's needs are reflected at all stages of policy formation and implementation.

Over the years, one of WEETU's most effective strategies has been to establish innovatory services which meet the needs of women, and which point the way to policy change to benefit other marginalised groups. For instance, a women-focused guidance service on training and educational opportunities piloted by WEETU has been extended and replicated by a range of mainstream providers, including local council education departments and Training and Enterprise Councils (TECs), and is now a central part of community level services in the area. Women who are outside the world of paid work have a wide range of relevant skills and experience. A government-sponsored Unpaid Work project showed how the skills women develop in the home, and in unpaid community work, are comparable to those required for National Vocational Qualifications in four occupational areas. The Project has developed a system for accreditation of unpaid work into the NVQ system.

The Full Circle Project

The Full Circle Project is a three-year pilot project to support women who want to set up their own microbusiness. A 'bundle' of resources is provided within the framework of the project: not only credit, but also business training, support, and appropriate levels of help with child care and transport problems. The project is designed to enhance the economic opportunities not only of the participants but also of their local communities, by increasing local economic activity, adding to local employment, providing positive role models, and building new networks of services.

The context

The project is based in three Norfolk communities: a council estate in Norwich, a declining agricultural community in north Norfolk, and a declining urban industrial area in the south of the county.

It is anticipated that about 225 women will be recruited from these three areas to take part in the enterprise training element of Full Circle. This starts with a pre-training familiarisation, an in-depth course entitled 'Is enterprise for me?', and a business-skills training module which includes business planning, financial and resource management, and marketing.

Transferring skills to other contexts

Not everyone is suited to business enterprise. Research in the USA leads us to predict that only 10 per cent of women initially recruited will pursue the programme to the final stage of taking a loan and setting up their own business.[3] However, the programme has been designed in line with WEETU's previous experience, so that skills and information developed at the pre-enterprise stages of the programme are transferable to other economic activities. If a woman chooses to take up training and educational opportunities or seek full- or part-time waged employment, we would regard this as a successful outcome of the project. The option of obtaining appropriate level NVQ and other accreditation is built into the planning of the training programmes.

Gaining group access to loans

A woman who opts for self-employment will become a member of a lending-business circle which will have access to loans for enterprise start-up expenses, and business and financial management training and advice. These circles will comprise four to six women, who will jointly assess each other's loan applications and be collectively liable for any individual default.

The lending circles will be responsible, with the support of Enterprise Development Officers, for establishing their own rules of operation, assessing the feasibility of individual businesses, and applying for loans. The loan fund will be managed by CAF (the Charities Aid Foundation). Loans will be fairly small (£500 or below) initially, but can be stepped up to a maximum of £2000. No credit checks are made on individuals; instead, as described above, the group takes on collective responsibility for repayment and for the possible defaults by any individual member. Therefore the groups will have to assess collectively the soundness of an individual woman's business plans, and whether she is likely to be a reliable repayer; repayment of a loan will be a prerequisite for others to borrow from the fund.

Those running successful businesses with sound repayment histories will have access to higher levels of credit; and it is anticipated that they will eventually progress to using financial and business services provided by the existing banking and business advice systems at the local and regional level.

The project is being run alongside another WEETU project, the Enterprising Women's Network, for established women entrepreneurs, which provides advice, mentoring, and business contacts for the 'proto-businesses' emerging from the Full Circle project.

Funding

The implementation of the project has been funded by the European Social Fund and the UK National Lottery Charities Board, This follows a developmental period which was supported by a range of funders, including some local funders.[4] The Charities Aid Foundation Loan Services have supported the development of the Loan Fund and a number of commercial banks are expected to participate in the future development of the programme.

Towards sustainability

In the context of Southern micro-credit schemes, sustainability has been seen from the institutional point of view and been concerned with rates of repayment, and whether income generated by fees and interest payment can cover transaction and administrative costs. But, while institutional sustainability is an important long-term goal, we take a different perspective, seeing sustainability in terms of the long-term sustainability of the individual woman participant and her household; and of WEETU's developing relationship with local partners and participation in policy debates on economic exclusion and strategies for poverty alleviation at both national and local levels.

Livelihood strategies and reducing risk

From the point of view of individual women, we need to ensure that the risk of investing their own time and resources in establishing a new business, from what many experts would see as an impossible starting position, does not threaten the security of their households. No rational woman would risk the survival of her household members by jeopardising income support to meet basic needs; therefore, women in low-income households can only be encouraged to initiate business ventures which offer income streams in the future if their families' immediate security is not threatened. As has been argued in the context of supporting women's businesses in developing countries, low-income households are not all in identical positions, and policies must be flexible enough to meet the particular circumstances of individuals and allow them to pursue micro-enterprises only when the security of their households has been met (Grown and Sebstad 1989).

We have therefore stressed to government that support for enterprise start-ups through microcredit and training can only form part of the new 'welfare to work' packages if carefully designed to meet the actual situation of low-income women (Pearson 1997). In our advocacy role we can make the case that the experience of this and other projects indicates that the government must recognise the need to share the risk with participants, and should allow for a gradual transition from benefits to independence, so that low-income women can make informed choices about their futures.

We are currently in discussions with the Department for Education and Employment, and the Department of Social Security, regarding a 'welfare waiver' for women presently living on benefits. This would allow women a period of 'enterprise rehearsal', during which subsistence and other benefit entitlements will be safeguarded. During that time, any surplus from trading can be re-channelled back into the business rather than being counted as income for living expenses. In this way entitlements to income support and associated benefits will be protected while the new microbusiness is nursed towards viability.[5]

These issues need to be discussed in the context of recognising that for many people the income from small businesses will for some time only partially cover living expenses (called 'income patching' in North America) but that the long-term benefits of building up experience in the mainstream economy, transferable skills, and connections with services and resources are positive outcomes; outright independence from welfare through self-supporting business activity should not be the only measure of success.

It is also mistaken to see sustainability for the project in terms of the ability to cover implementation and transaction costs from the interest generated by financial services. The UK government has already conceded this point in an agreement concluded in 1994 with the Prince's Youth Business Trust (an organisation that provides business credit for disadvantaged young people). Under this scheme the Department for Education and Employment grants a payment of £1500 to the PYBT for each unemployed participant whose business is still trading 15 months after start up; a payment which helps to meet the running cost of the organisation (Hayday and Locke 1997).

Here, the government has recognised that sustainability should be understood in terms of successful outcomes for participants, rather than of covering project costs.

For WEETU, long-term sustainability needs to be seen in other ways. We need to maintain and develop our relationship with partners in the communities with whom we work, and in the policy arenas of the region, so that the lessons from our pilot projects can be built into to policy options for the whole country. For instance, we would like to see support for new microenterprises as being part of the Government's New Deal for Youth and Long Term Unemployed. We would argue that any schemes to promote employment at the community level should recognise the need to offer part-time as well as full-time work, if women (and others) are going to be able to re-connect to the world of training and work.

We need to work with other organisations to develop parallel microfinance services in the communities in which we work. In particular we would like to see developments in the provision of credit for consumption and community activities, as well as an extension of the savings and barter services currently offered by Credit Unions and LETS (Local Exchange Trading Schemes).

We need to explore ways in which the scale of business credit can be increased, and members of low-income communities enabled to use mainstream banking and financial services. Our project should demonstrate to a historically sceptical banking industry that people on low incomes do not necessarily have low prospects and that it is worthwhile for banks to develop an appropriate range of services for these people.

However, at the same time an important principle for the Full Circle Project is to maintain a focus on loans for low-income groups, and to resist the pressure to move towards financial sustainability by diversifying into more profitable, larger loans. Hence the stress on developing mechanisms through which our successful participants can make the transition to using the financial services of mainstream banks, leaving us to concentrate on other women wishing to start up businesses.

Conclusions

There has been a much debate about the assumption that credit for women can empower them — either in economic terms (Mayoux 1997) or more widely. Despite the tendency among many donors to see credit as a universal remedy for women's poverty, our international development experience has made us painfully aware of the problems and pitfalls of using credit as a 'one-size-fits-all' approach.

However, there is another issue which arises in this context. The 1997 Microcredit Summit organised by *RESULTS* was hailed by Northern government spokespersons, including Hillary Clinton, as a global strategy for poverty eradication. Development agencies and experts with experience in the South should beware of importing uncritically models developed and refined in the South to the very different context of poverty and social exclusion in the North. Women's poverty in Northern countries has to be seen within the context of structural changes in labour market supply and demand factors and in the relationships between employment and welfare systems. Individual projects have to be designed in the context of such systems, and involve a dialogue with policy-makers and implementers.

WEETU's Full Circle Project is a response by a women's organisation to the dynamics of women's poverty and economic exclusion in contemporary Britain. We have developed this 'credit-plus' approach on the basis of our experience with women in the local economy. The success of the Full Circle Project will depend as much on its contribution to the reconsideration of the causes and dynamics of women's poverty in Britain as its provision of examples of successful women-run businesses and loan repayments.

Ruth Pearson is a founder Chair of WEETU and the Full Circle Steering Committee. She teaches Gender and Development at the School of Development Studies, University of East Anglia, and the Institute of Sociaal Studies at the Hague.

Erika Watson is Coordinator of WEETU and Director of the Full Circle Fund Project. She has carried out research into the potential of the Grameen Bank model for poor communities in the North.

Notes

1 'Real wages' refers to the actual purchasing power of wages, taking into account price inflation.
2 'Welfare-to-work' is a term denoting policy measures to enable people living in poverty to move from welfare to income generation.
3 In May 1997 the authors visited group credit projects in low-income neighbourhoods in Chicago and Boston, and attended the conference of the Association of Economic Opportunities at which some hundreds of microcredit and finance projects in the ISA were represented.
4 These include WEETU's core funders, Norwich City Council as well as the Allen Lane Foundation, Oxfam UK/NI, the Gulbenkian Foundation, the Rural Development Council and the Norfolk and Waveney Training and Enterprise Council.
5 The previous UK government ran a programme under which people were paid a small stipend for 12 months (called an Enterprise Allowance) whilst they developed their business ideas. This national scheme was discontinued some years ago. In the United States, since *Self-Employment Exemption,* which became law in 1992, entrepreneurs are allowed two years to build their businesses while still receiving their benefits, though each state can decide the length and conditions of this exemption. To qualify they have to participate in a recognised enterprise programme and provide the appropriate state office with records of the financial transactions of their business. See for example WSEP 1995 which describes the regulations for a scheme in the State of Illinois.

References

Balls, E (1993) 'Danger: Men not at work' in Balls, E and Gregg, P, *Work and Welfare: Tackling the Jobs deficit* London, Institute for Public Policy Research.

Goetz, A M and Sen Gupta, R (1996) 'Who takes the credit? Gender, power and control over loan use in rural credit programmes in Bangladesh', *World Development* 24: 1, pp 45–63.

Gregg, P and Wadsworth, J (1995) 'A short history of labour turnover, job tenure and job security, 1975–93', *Oxford Review of Economic Policy* 11:1.

Grown, C and Sebstad, J (1989) 'Introduction: towards a wider perspective on women's employment' *World Development* 17: 7.

Hayday, M and Locke, M (1997) 'Social Investment and Microfinance'; paper given at the Development Studies Association Conference, UEA, Norwich September.

MacFarlane, R (1997) *Unshackling the Poor: A Complementary Approach to Local Economic Development* Joseph Rowntree Foundation, York.

Mayoux, L (1997) 'Women's empowerment and micro-finance programmes: approaches, evidence and ways forward'; Draft Overview Paper for Pilot Project: 'Micro Finance Programmes and Women's Empowerment: Strategies for Increasing Impact' July

Pearson, R (1997) 'Credit for micro-entrepreneurs: issues relating to policies on welfare to work and local economic development', mimeo, May, School of Development Studies, UEA, Norwich.

WSEP (1995) *Self-Employment: A Guide for AFDC Recipients*, The Women's Self Employment Project (WSEP) Chicago.

Building community capacity:

Hull and East Yorkshire PRA Network

Tilly Sellers

Participatory Rural Appraisal (PRA) is a powerful and productive approach which enables communities to analyse their situation and mobilise for action. In East Yorkshire, PRA training offered to local people led to the formation of a network of practitioners and community activists.

In 1995, the Department of Public Health Medicine at the University of Hull was able to offer Participatory Rural Appraisal[1] (PRA) training to local residents and community-based workers, as part of a local health authority funded project on teenage sexual health. A number of those trained became practitioners in their own communities, and PRA quickly became recognised as a powerful approach to both urban and rural social development in the area. A network was formed and there was further demand for training from local community activists. Between the beginning of 1996 and June 1997, over 130 people participated in PRA training. The majority were community-based workers, predominantly from the voluntary sector, with an increasing number of requests from residents' groups and from statutory field workers. Working with disadvantaged groups, some 30 community-led PRA projects were initiated, covering a wide range of issues including drugs, violence, service provision, health, the environment, poverty, and general capacity-building.

Initially administered by University workers, the PRA Network underwent an almost organic growth, moving in a self-directed way to meet needs and tackle issues as they came up. Meeting monthly, the first focus was on mutual support. Then began the process of acquainting peers, and those in more powerful positions, with the principle of community participation, and PRA techniques. This happened quite quickly, as more work was carried out within communities, and some (although not all) began to see the usefulness of this approach.

The Network also served to encourage personal development. The PRA training is accredited through the Open College Network. Several people were able to add their PRA practice to their CVs, enabling them to obtain jobs, or take further education courses. The Network meetings became a safe, equitable opportunity to share ideas for tools and projects, and eventually became a forum for sharing work. It is now acceptable practice for people from a variety of backgrounds to form PRA teams, and to collaborate on projects. This began on a voluntary basis, but more recently some projects have attracted funding, and those not in employment can sometimes receive payment for their work.

As the number of Network members grew, there reached a critical point and a recognition that they had become a fairly powerful group with a high level of networking and collaboration between agencies, and between the voluntary and statutory sectors and the community. At this point the idea of gaining financial support for the Network in its own right was mooted. This resulted in support from Oxfam's UK Anti-Poverty Programme, and in tasks being shared out amongst Network members. The Network was able to become independent from the University. Training, information and fundraising were given priority (see below for contacts). A number of successful funding applications were made for different projects, including a three-year project, working with marginalised young people in rural areas, which received a grant from the National Lottery Charitable Fund. Hull Council for Voluntary Service also arranged to support the PRA training costs of resident groups.

It was at this point that the Network identified its shared philosophy (although recognising that this is likely to change as the Network evolves). The emphasis is clearly on development rather than on research. PRA is defined by the Network as: *attitudes, behaviour and tools to enable a community-driven process of social, physical and income regeneration amongst disadvantaged groups.*

Aims of the Network

Aims and objectives of the PRA Netowrk currently include:

- To provide PRA training locally and nationally, with the emphasis on fee payers subsidising free training for residents and community groups.
- To provide information about PRA locally and nationally through a central contact.

- To provide free or subsidised PRA facilitation where requested by community initiatives with an emphasis on community capacity-building and giving a voice to those who traditionally go unheard.
- To provide free or subsidised consultation to community groups wishing to carry out participatory projects of their own which combat inequity and deprivation.
- To provide opportunities for skill sharing and exchange of cultures with PRA practitioners from the South.

There are many types of PRA projects facilitated by Network members; there is room here to include just one example of a project in progress. After PRA training with residents and workers in one area, a request was received by the Network from residents through a local domestic violence forum. A small amount of funding was available, and they wanted an appraisal of perceptions, issues and service needs to be carried out on a particular housing estate. A group of residents and workers from the estate agreed to participate in PRA training. Working with diverse groups on the estate, they will go on to focus their fieldwork on the causes, and impact, of domestic violence. Network members will then help them to appraise service needs. A review of national project work on domestic violence is also being produced by the Network. This is intended to stimulate ideas, and to highlight examples of good practice. The Domestic Violence Forum will assist by linking resident's groups to sources of funding where necessary.

PRA is a powerful and productive approach, and this is, without doubt, the main reason for its swift uptake in disadvantaged areas of the North. There may, however, be additional reasons for its success. Conversely, the limitations and risks of PRA and this type of networking are currently unknown, and have so far not become apparent in Hull and East Yorkshire. A participatory process evaluation of the Network is clearly needed, which may give some indications of the effects and impact of the PRA Network. It may also give some insight into critical conditions necessary for its replication elsewhere. In 1997, further research funding from the NHS Executive enabled PRA training to be held in Walsall and in Wester Hailes in Edinburgh, where similar networks are beginning to be established.

Tilly Sellers can be contacted at the Department of Public Health Medicine, University of Hull, Hull HU6 7RX.
Tel: 01482 466056 Fax: 01482 441408
email: P.Sellers@phm.hull.ac.uk

Notes

1 PRA is an approach that combines education with research and collective action. Participants use mainly visual tools (for example, mapping and diagramming) to enable them to move through a process of looking at their current situation, and identifying areas for change. They verify this information through 'triangulation' — i.e. cross-checking the conclusions through using different analytical tools, and constant feedback. This process is repeated with a wide range of stakeholder groups, in order to examine the diversity of opinion and need within a self-defined community. Through a process of dialogue, action is then prioritised, planned, implemented and monitored by participants themselves (Chambers, 1994).

Hull and East Yorkshire PRA Network contacts

Information: Linda Tock, Community Focus, Hull Education Centre, Coronation Road North, Hull HU5 5RL. Tel: 01482 883783

Email pranet@comfocus.karoo.co.uk

Training: Paul Spooner, Hull DoC, 154–155 Highcourt, Orchard Park, Hull HU6 9YS Tel: 01482 854550

Finance: Roger Newton, Rural Community Council for Humber and Wolds, 14 Market Place, Howden DN14 7BJ. Tel: 01430 430904

Wester Hailes: Lynn Wotherspoon, 10/1 Dumbryden Grove, Edinburgh EH14 2QW. Tel: 0131 5387028

Walsall: Daren Garratt, Eleanor Chell, WALKWAYS, 44 Littleton Street West, Walsall, WS2 8EW. Tel: 01922 721805

References

Chambers, R (1994) 'The Origins and Practice of Participatory Rural Appraisal' *World Development* Vol. 22, No. 7, pp. 953–969

INTERVIEW

Helen Carmichael

LEAP Theatre Workshop

Interviewed by Nicky May

Where does the name of your organisation come from?
In the words of Alec Davison, a member of LEAP: 'our name sums up the fact that to make a leap is a creative act that sparks the resolving of conflict. It is a leap of faith, since we leap in the dark. We plunge from the known of the hurt, to the unknown of how it may be healed.'

How did LEAP's work start?
The concept of LEAP Confronting Conflict, our conflict-resolution training programme, evolved from the work of LEAP theatre workshop, which was set up in 1987 by Leaveners, the Quaker performing arts charity. The theatre workshop was initiated in response to growing youth unemployment. Its aim was to encourage young people under pressure to explore the causes of and alternatives to conflict, through drama and theatre.

Having toured participatory theatre-workshops nation-wide, performing in youth, community, and penal venues, and established a reputation for its vigorous issues-based workshop style, LEAP then aimed to deepen its training work in addressing issues of conflict, violence and mediation.

What sort of issues facing young men and women does LEAP's work address?
We work with whichever issues young people bring into our activities working on conflict. These are often conflicts in personal relationships, for example, conflicts with their parents, or their brothers and sisters, or conflicts with their children if they are parents. Sometimes the conflicts involve institutions — for example, breaking the rules or bullying at school, or getting into trouble with the police. Sometimes the conflicts arise out of lack of resources caused by poverty, unemployment or racism. Our emphasis is on seeing young people as creators, problem solvers and leaders.

How did you go about designing the anti-conflict training?
The techniques and structure of learning grew in an original LEAP style, which suggests that young people should welcome the opportunity that conflict brings, even

though it is also dangerous. Coming to terms with conflict, and using it creatively, leads to personal growth.

A 60-hour training module was developed, learning from many other organisations in the field. This stemmed from action research in Britain, America, Europe, Australia, and New Zealand. We developed a theoretical framework, which includes a synthesis of communication, affirmation, assertiveness, anger management, team building, and mediation skills, experienced through drama, role play, and enactive group work.

LEAP plays with the concept of fire, to help to analyse the causes and escalation of conflict. For young people, fire is a more dynamic concept than peace. The training team makes accessible to young people a pattern of practical strategies, and rehearses a 'fire drill', to help both youth workers and young people to cope creatively with everyday conflicts. The content of the sessions is different in each workshop, as it arises from the everyday situations of the participants.

In 1992 LEAP published a training manual based on this concept for professional youth workers, *Playing with Fire*, and a handbook for those working with young people, *Fireworks*. A pack of discussion posters — *Burning Issues* — is published by the Leaveners Press.

What are the objectives of LEAP Confronting Conflict?
The LEAP Confronting Conflict Project was formed to provide further exploration of conflict, and training, for both professional youth workers and young volunteers working with young people on the issue, and to generate new projects and programmes of work with young people.

Could you describe your current activities?
We run our own courses to train young volunteers in mediation and conflict resolution techniques — they will go on to work in the community, with their peers

and alongside adults. We focus a lot on working 'youth to youth', and hope to encourage young people who would not normally volunteer, to join us.

We provide a range of training courses based on our action research for professionals in the youth, social, community and prison services. Courses are led by members of LEAP's pool of freelance trainers, who come from drama, education, and youth social work backgrounds. We provide information on the models we use through training manuals and publications, and evaluation documents. We also have a consultancy/training programme designing short courses, mainly one or two days, for organisations throughout the UK.

LEAP Islington is a project run in association with Islington Youth Service in London, for volunteers interested in training in work with young people in conflict. Part-time training in conflict resolution and facilitation skills is offered to 12–16 volunteers followed by a six-month supported placement, one evening a week, in a range of local youth clubs.

Recent peer-education projects in schools in the London Boroughs of Tower Hamlets and Camden have resulted in two publications. *Tackling Bullying: Conflict Resolution with Young People* is a manual of materials designed to provide ideas for activities though which young people aged twelve years and over can explore the issues involved in bullying behaviour. *Promoting Positive Behaviour: Activities for Preventing Bullying in Primary Schools* is a pack for work with children under twelve years.

Finally, there's the *Quarrel Shop*, our most experimental piece of work yet. It is a programme which aims to enable young people to take responsibility for resolving their own disputes, to tackle bullying and violence for themselves, and make creative use of the conflicts in their lives. To do this, mediation skills are taught. This communications process encourages young people to sort out their problems with someone closer to their own age. Additional training is given in facilitation, community support, and leadership. Over the past three years we have run projects in a variety of youth service venues. Over the next two years, a young people's mediation and conflict-resolution service will be created. Various projects will also take place in the community, in particular, with the mediation services of north-east London, as well as youth clubs and at national recognised conferences.

Can you describe LEAP's work with young offenders[1]?
We are working with HMP (Her Majesty's Prison) Feltham Young Offenders' Institution and Remand Centre, with the support of the Sir John Cass's Foundation, on coping with conflicts and anger management. We are also developing a training module for use in other Young Offenders' institutions, and for work with young men who are at risk of offending.

We encourage inmates to use their time on remand to reflect on their lives and make changes. We run three-day workshops, using drama and role-play, using the participants'

own life stories as our starting point. We look at cycles of violence, and the points at which they could potentially 'step off'. We start the young men off on a search for changes and encourage the staff to support the changes that the prisoners choose to make. Short-term evaluation shows that the young men enjoy the work; their self-esteem increases, and their tendency to use violence decreases after taking part. As with any changes that we choose to make, they do need support in the longer term from other organisations to keep going with the positive alternatives they are trying out. We know we act as a spark for most to try something new'.

LEAP Confronting Conflict can be contacted at The LAB, 8 Lennox Road, Finsbury Park, London N4 3NW, UK.
Tel: 00 44 171 272 5630

Notes

1 Young offenders have been found guilty of criminal activity

Delegates at The Third Young People and Conflict Conference 1996

Frank Herrmann

Resources

compiled by Sara Chamberlain

Further reading

Books

Poverty: The Facts, Carey Oppenheim and Lisa Harker, Child Poverty Action Group , 1996
Poverty: The Facts is a comprehensive and authoritative assessment of poverty in the UK. It gives the latest poverty figures for the UK, provides comparative statistics on poverty in Europe, and reveals the extent of income and regional inequalities.

The Welfare State: Putting the Record Straight, by Carey Oppenheim, Child Poverty Action Group, 1994
This analysis of the welfare state in the UK denies government claims that social security spending will outpace economic growth in future years. It also covers issues such as race, homelessness, health and the sexual politics of deprivation.

Living and Working: An Illustration of the Feminisation of Poverty in Europe, Network Women in Development Europe (WIDE), 1995
A collection of case studies that relate the feminisation of poverty in Europe to the failure of the current development model. Economic globalisation makes it essential to trace the links between women's experiences all over the world.

Women and Poverty in Britain: The 1990s, edited by Caroline Glendinning and Jane Millar, Harvester Wheatsheaf, 1992
A fully revised and updated edition of the classic text. It analyses the extent of women's poverty in a variety of contexts and social roles and how women are managing poverty on a daily basis. The most comprehensive and up-to-date analysis of the causes, extent and consequences of women's poverty in Britain.

Faces of Poverty: Portraits of Women and Children on Welfare, Jill Duerr Berrick, Oxford University Press, 1995
Most Americans are insulated from the poor. Instead, they are exposed to rhetoric and hyperbole about the excesses of the American welfare system. These messages close the American mind to a full understanding of the complexity of family poverty. But who are these poor families? What do we know about how they arrived in such desperate straits? Is poverty their fate for a lifetime or only for a brief period? In *Faces of Poverty*, Jill Duerr Berrick answers these questions as she dispels misconceptions and myths about welfare and the welfare population in America.

America's Struggle Against Poverty 1900–1994, James T Patterson, Harvard University Press, 1995
In this probing history of twentieth-century American attitudes toward the poor, James Patterson explores how Americans have

viewed poverty and what their welfare reformers have tried to do about it. Broad in its scope, the book is especially pertinent to the welfare-reform debate of the 1990s.

Life on a low income, Elaine Kempson, Joseph Rowntree Foundation, 1996. The Homestead, 40 Water End, York YO3 6LP. Elaine Kempson argues that people living on low incomes in the UK are not an under-class, but share the same aspirations as others in society. This book paints a vivid picture of life on a low income and shows how social, economic, and policy changes could make that life less difficult.

The Oxfam Poverty Report, Kevin Watkins, Oxfam UK and Ireland, 1995
Based on case studies and examples from Oxfam's experience in over 70 countries, this report examines the causes of poverty and conflict. It concludes by proposing some of the policy and institutional reforms which would lead to an environment where people can act as agents of change to reduce poverty.

The Dynamics of Poverty, James Williams and Brendan Whelan, Combat Poverty Agency, 1994 . The Bridgewater Centre, Conyngham Road, Islandbridge, Dublin 8.
Draws on information from large-scale sample surveys to show that Irish households experience changes in their poverty status over time, and therefore the notion of a fixed and relatively unchanging stock of households below the poverty line must be revised.

Lone Parents: Poverty and Public Policy in Ireland, Jane Millar, Sandra Leeper, and Celia Davies, Combat Poverty Agency, 1992
By 1989, there were at least 40,000 lone-parent families in Ireland, the vast majority headed by women. Lone-parent families have a much higher risk of poverty. This study represents a major contribution to the understanding of poverty, as experienced by lone parents. It examines employment, maintenance and social welfare in comparison with provisions in other countries.

The Exclusive Society: Citizenship and the Poor, Ruth Lister, Child Poverty Action Group
Ruth Lister argues that poverty excludes millions from the full rights of citizenship, undermining their ability to fulfil either their private or social obligations. She demonstrates that it is impossible to divorce the rights and responsibilities which are supposed to unite citizens from the inequalities of power and resources that divide them.

A Poor Future, Peter Townsend, Lemos and Crane in association with The Friendship Group, 1996
Professor Townsend concisely and accessibly reveals disturbing new trends in the twin evils of poverty and social polarisation across the globe and in Britain. He proposes a new strategy to stop greater polarisation and stabilise living standards, which takes into account global economics. In a mixed economy greater priority has to be given to innovations within the public sector as well as the restoration of the principles of public service.

Paying for Inequality: The Economic Cost of Social Injustice, Andrew Glyn and David Miliban (eds), IPPR/Rivers Oram Press, 1994
Confronts the basic assumption that measures to promote equality always incur a cost in economic efficiency. In fact, inequality in Britain today is a barrier to economic success. Includes papers by 15 experts in health, labour economics, education, social policy, taxation and criminology.

Poverty: Answering Back,
Oxfam UK/I and Channel Four
Poverty: Answering Back is a collection of testimonies from people living in poverty around the world. Each story is accompanied by statistical 'poverty/wealth indicators' for the particular part of the world, brief background information on the causes of the relevant form of poverty and some of the agencies involved in relieving it.

Unfair Share: The effects of widening social differences on the welfare of the young, R G Wilkinson, Barnardo's, 1994. Tanner Lane, Barkingside, Ilford, IG6 1Q6.
Wide ranging-analysis covering health, crime, homelessness, suicide and drug abuse in the context of absolute poverty and relative deprivation.

Challenging Assumptions: Gender Considerations in Urban Regeneration in the United Kingdom, A Report to the Joseph Rowntree Foundation, Nicky May, JRF, 1997
Significant growth in unemployment, particularly for unskilled labour; the entry of women into the formal labour market; the casual, low-paid and part-time jobs, availble to women; and changes in family structure have had a major impact on gender relations, roles and identities, not just in the workplace, but within the home and community. This report sets out to understand these changes and identify ways of addressing the problems of changing gender roles.

Articles and pamphlets:

The myths of dependence and self-sufficiency: Women, welfare and low-wage work, Kathryn J. Edin, Rutgers University
Based on interview data from 214 AFDC recipients and 165 low-wage workers in four US cities.

Welfare that works: the working lives of AFDC recipients, a report to the Ford Foundation by the Institute of Women's Policy Research
Explores the complex realities of work and welfare among mothers receiving Aid to Families with Dependent Children in America.

Rising Tide, Sinking Wages, Lawrence Mishel, The American Prospect No 23, 1995
Examines why the living standards of the broad middle class have remained in continuous decline in the US despite the robust performance of the economy.

Recent Wage Trends: The Implications for Low Wage Workers, Gary Burtless and Lawrence Mishel, prepared for the Social Science Research Council Policy Conference on Persistent Urban Poverty, 1993
Discusses increasing wage inequality in America during the last two decades, and the changes in wage structure that have led to an increasing number of workers earning low and very low wages.

How can they be poor — they've all got videos!, Child Poverty Action Group, 1994
Explodes myths about poverty in the UK, including 'There isn't any poverty in the UK', 'The poor don't want to work, they're lazy and expect wages which are too high', 'Benefit levels are adequate to live on'.

Myths about food and low income,
The National Food Alliance, 5–11 Worship Street, london EC2A 2BH.
Explodes the myths such as: 'This isn't Africa. Nobody is going short of food', 'Healthy food isn't expensive', 'If you give them more money, they just spend it on fags or the lottery', and 'If they don't eat a healthy diest it's their own fault.'

Newsletters and journals

Focus
Newsletter of the Institute of Poverty Research, University of Wisconsin. Publishes research into the causes and consequences of poverty and social inequality in the United States.

Poverty Research News
The newsletter of the Northwestern University/ University of Chicago Joint Center for Poverty Research. Frequently covers issues relating to women and poverty in the North. Available online at:
http://www.spc.uchicago.edu/wwwusr/o rgs/povcen/summer97/index.html

Organisations

UK

Oxfam UK and Ireland Poverty Programme
In 1994 Oxfam began to gather information about poverty in the UK. It was clear that the number of individuals living in poverty, and the level of inequality, had increased substantially since the 1970 — as have poor health, poor housing, homelessness and unemployment. Oxfam's UK Poverty Programme emphasizes sharing experiences and skills from around the world, and seeks to strengthen social organisations and capacity-building within groups marginalised by poverty. It also works to influence attitudes to poverty; address links between race, poverty and exclusion; and strengthen the analysis of poverty through the introduction of an international perspective. The programme puts particular emphasis on issues of poverty and gender.
UK Poverty Programme
274 Banbury Road,
Oxford, OX2 7DZ
Tel. (44) (0)1865 311 311

Child Poverty Action Group (CPAG)
Aims to promote action for the relief, direct or indirect, of poverty among UK children and families. Provides welfare benefits advice and training for advisers, reaerch into family poverty issues, and public information and campaigns on children's welfare and rights.
CPAG, 4th floor,
1–5 Bath Street, London EC1V 9PY
Tel: (44) (0)171 253 3406
Fax: (0)171 490 0561

Crisis
A UK national charity for single homeless people — i.e. those with no statutory right to housing. Researches, develops and funds schemes to provide help when most needed, at whatever stage of homelessness, from emergency help on the streets through to hostels, permanent housing and resettlement support.

7 Whitechapel Road
London E1 1DU
Tel: (44) (0)171 377 0489
Fax: (44) (0)171 247 1525

Akina Mama wa Afrika
Works for African women in the UK, Europe and Africa, and is involved with community development, advocacy and counselling.
4 Wild Court,
London WC2B 5AH
Tel: (44) (0)171 405 0678

Single Parent Action Network
A national, multi-racial UK organisation run by single parents and set up in 1990 as part of the Third European Poverty Programme. Works to improve policies and practices for single parents and their children in Britain, and to support self-help groups in different parts of the country. Workers and volunteers in the network support over 1,000 groups in the UK, and work to change policy and practice that discriminates against one-parent families.
Single Parent Action Network
Millpond, Baptist Street,
Easton, Bristol, BS5 OYJ

Food Poverty Network
Provides a regular newsletter, a comprehensive database of food poverty projects, regional conferences, and contacts for those working in the field.
National Food Alliance (NFA)
5-11 Worship Street, London EC2A 2BH
Tel: (44) (0)171 628 2442
Fax: (44) (0)171 628 9329

ATD Fourth World
Aims to break down the ostracism endured by the poor and to develop public awareness of poverty. Projects include family respite stays, street workshops and citizenship forums in the UK and abroad.
48 Addington Square
London SE5 7LB
Tel: (44) (0)171 703 3231
Fax: (44) (0)171 252 4276

Barnardo's
Has 200 services annually working with 26,500 children, young people and families in local communities, helping them tackle poverty, homelessness, HIV/AIDS and sexual abuse.
Tanners Lane, Barkingside,
Ilford, Essex 1G6 1QG
Tel: (44) (0)181 550 8822
Fax: (44) (0)181 551 6870

Family Welfare Association (FWA)
Assists families and individuals to overcome poverty in tangible ways, providing practical, emotional and financial support. Runs family and children's centres, provides community mental health care and administers trust funds.
501–505 Kingsland Road,
London E8 4AU
Tel: (44) (0)171 254 6251
Fax: (44) (0)171 249 5443

Low Pay Unit
Leading organisation highlighting and investigating problems related to poverty. Investigates and publicises low pay, poverty and related issues, stimulates debate and provides advice and information for employers and low-paid workers. Lobbies government and MPs, and provides reports and information on low-pay issues, as well as a rights service and training on rights-related issues.
27–29 Amwell Street,
London EC1 1UN
Tel: (44) (0)171 713 7616
Fax: (44) (0)171 713 7581

The Poverty Alliance
Seeks to combat poverty in Scotland through the promotion of strategic and collaborative action. Activities include awareness raising, network development, publications, project development and support, and skills training for community leaders who are active in local anti-poverty initatives.
162 Buchanan Street,
Glasgow G1 2ll
Tel: (44) (0)141 353 0440
Fax: (44) (0)141 353 0686

The Institute for Women's Policy Research (IWPR)
An independent, nonprofit, research organisation founded in 1987. IWPR works for policymakers, scholars, and advocacy groups to design, execute, and disseminate research findings on policy issues affecting women and families.
1400 20th Street NW, Suite 104, Washington DC 20036.

Western Europe

Network Women in Development Europe (WIDE)
Established in 1985, WIDE is composed of 15 national platforms of women's organisations and individuals working on international issues. It works to influence European and international policies to raise awareness on gender and development issues among important sectors of opinion in Europe, with the objective of empowering women worldwide. WIDE carries out specific actions, networking and lobbying on concrete issues, jointly with women living in the South, and research on women and poverty in the North.
WIDE, Square Ambiorix, 10
1040 Brussels — Belgium
Tel. 32-2-732-44-10
Fax 32-2-732-19-34

North America

The Northwestern University / University of Chicago Joint Center for Poverty Research
Supports academic research that focuses on the causes of poverty and the effectiveness of policies aimed at reducing poverty. Areas of research include: changing labor markets and the causes of inequality in the current labor market; family functioning and the well-being of children; the impact of concentrated urban poverty; and the effects of changing policy and new programs. Facilitates the

collection of new data, including state administrative data, that will be critical for future advances in poverty research.
Northwestern University Institute for Policy Research
2046 Sheridan Road
Evanston, IL 60208 USA
Phone: 847-491-4145
Fax: 847-467-2459

Institute of Poverty Research

A national, university-based centre for research into the causes and consequences of poverty and social inequality in the United States. It is nonprofit and nonpartisan. Established in 1966 at the University of Wisconsin-Madison by the US Office of Economic Opportunity, the Institute's multidisci-plinary affiliates have formulated and tested theories of poverty and inequality, developed and evaluated social policy alternatives, and analysed trends in poverty and economic well-being
3412 Social Science Building
1180 Observatory Drive
Madison, WI 53706 USA
Telephone Numbers: (608) 262-6358
(608) 265-3119 (FAX)
E-mail: evanson@ssc.wisc.edu..

The Institute for Children and Poverty

The Institute for Children and Poverty — the research arm of Homes for the Homeless — provides innovative strategies to combat the impact of homelessness and urban poverty on the lives of children and their families through the development of effective public policy initiatives and the dissemination of quantitative research findings.
hn4061@handsnet.org
Homes for the Homeless
36 Cooper Square, 6th Floor
New York, NY 10003 USA
Phone: 212-529-5252
Fax: 212-529-7698

Share Our Strength

Works to alleviate and prevent hunger and poverty in the United States and around the world, by supporting food assistance, treating malnutrition and other consequences of hunger, and promoting economic independence among people in need. SOS mobilizes industries and individuals to contribute their talents and creates community wealth to promote lasting change.Telephone 1-800-969-4767.

The Ontario Coalition Against Poverty

Seeks to eliminate 'poor-bashing' and poverty in Ontario, Canada, and the world. Also seeks to empower people who are in poverty, to stand up for their rights.
Global Community Centre:
Phone: (519) 746-4090
FAX: (519) 746-4096
E-mail: gccwat@web.net

Australia

Taskforce on Poverty

A taskforce on poverty has been established by Western Australia's Family and Children's Services Minister Cheryl Edwardes as part of the International Year for the Eradication of Poverty, to contribute to Western Australia's response to IYEP by developing an innovative plan to initiate research, debate and action by all sectors of the community.
Central Office East Perth WA 6004 Australia
Tel (08) 9222 2555
Fax (08) 9222 2776

Campaigns

National Dialogue on Poverty campaign
The National Association of Community Action Agencies (NACAA)

A campaign to bring the voices of low-income citizens into the debate on poverty in America. Plans include a nationwide series of local dialogues about poverty — its causes and effects as well as ways to combat it. Each dialogue will involve people with low incomes and other community leaders

in an open discussion about the realities of poverty. The information will be synthesized into state and regional summaries.
MACA,
2410 Hyde Park Road, Suite B,
Jefferson City, MO 65109, USA
Tel: (1) (573) 643 2969

The National Women's March Against Poverty

A country-wide march for jobs and justice initiated by the National ActionCommittee on the Status of Women (NAC) and the Canadian Labour Congress (CLC) to raise awareness about the impact of federal government cuts on women's lives in Canada.
http://www.women.ca/womens-march/#what

Web Sites

The HungerWeb

The aim of this site is to help eradicate hunger by facilitating the free exchange of ideas and information on the causes of, and solutions to, hunger. Contains information, made available by the World Hunger Program and its partners, as well as links to other sites where relevant information can be found.
http://www.brown.edu/Departments/World_Hunger_Program/

The Economic Policy Institute

A nonprofit, nonpartisan think tank that seeks to broaden the public debate about strategies to achieve a prosperous and fair economy. Includes academic research papers on the economic causes of poverty, as well as a large on-line library.
http://www.epinet.org/

Handsnet

Linking the human service community on-line, HandsNet is a national, nonprofit organisation that promotes information sharing, cross-sector collaboration and advocacy among individuals and organisations working on a broad range of public interest issues, including poverty. Includes articles, discussion forums and on-line membership information.
http://www.handsnet.org

Joint Center for Poverty Research

(see under organisations)
http://www.spc.uchicago.edu/wwwusr/orgs/pvecen/index.html

Share our Strength

(see under organisations)
http://www.strength.org/sosinfo.html

Institute for Research on Poverty

(see under organisations)
http://www.ssc.wisc.edu/irp/home.html

The Coalition For The Homeless

The nation's oldest and most progressive organisation helping homeless men, women, and children. Dedicated to the principle that decent shelter, affordable housing, sufficient food, and the chance to work for a living wage are fundamental rights. Includes information on the organisation's services, news and events, and how people can help the homeless.
http://www.homeless.24x7.com/index.htm

Index to Volume 5

Listings

Book Review